MULTIPLE INTELLIGENCES AND ADULT LITERACY: A SOURCEBOOK FOR PRACTITIONERS

What Adult Educators Have to Say About
Multiple Intelligences and Adult Literacy: A Sourcebook for Practitioners

This information, and approach to helping teachers go beyond traditional lessons, is so exciting. Our students are so diverse and their needs so great. Thanks for all the ideas.

Sharon Feyedelem, Adult Basic Education and Literacy Coordinator,
Sandusky City Schools, Ohio

I liked the collaborative tone of the text, meaning the researchers spoke to me, engaged me in their thinking and work. I wanted to return to it. . . . This material gave me new tools and language I wasn't using before. . . . The ironic thing is, what we in my program try to teach our students is that young children learn through play: Dramatic play, reading books, building towers, singing songs, touch, experimentation. If I want my students to value that kind of teaching and learning for their children, I have to model it everywhere, not just with their children while they are in the program, but in the adult classroom too!

Marie Kennedy, Family Literacy Teacher,
Family and Youth Services Bureau, Valparaiso, IN

Multiple Intelligences and Adult Literacy helped me shape the questions in ways that allowed for interpersonal and intrapersonal intelligences to work. I had asked people to use those intelligences before (although I didn't call them that), but had thought of those questions as "frills."

Kate Nonesuch, Literacy Coordinator, Reading Writing Centre,
Malaspina University, Duncan, BC, Canada

I got a lot of creative ideas from the Sourcebook along with justifications and concrete reasons for their success.

Trish Rowland, ABE Resource Teacher,
Department of Career and Community Education, West Palm Beach, FL

MULTIPLE INTELLIGENCES AND ADULT LITERACY: A SOURCEBOOK FOR PRACTITIONERS

Julie Viens & Silja Kallenbach

Foreword by Howard Gardner

TEACHERS COLLEGE PRESS

Teachers College, Columbia University
New York and London

52271433

3-15-04

Published by Teachers College Press
1234 Amsterdam Avenue
New York, NY 10027

Library of Congress Cataloging-in-Publication Data
Viens, Julie
    Multiple intelligences and adult literacy : a sourcebook for practitioners /
Julie Viens and Silja Kallenbach ; foreword by Howard Gardner
      p.   cm.
    ISBN 0-8077-4346-1 (pbk.)
    Includes bibliographical references and index.
    1. Functional literacy. 2. Multiple intelligences. 3. Learning strategies.
  I. Kallenbach, Silja. II. Title
  LC149.7 .M85 2003   2003054027
  302.2/244 21

For more information contact:
Project Zero
Harvard Graduate School of Education
124 Mount Auburn Street, Suite 500
Cambridge, Massachusetts 02138
(617) 495-4342
http://pzweb.harvard.edu
info@pz.harvard.edu

NCSALL
Harvard Graduate School of Education
7 Appian Way, 101 Nichols House
Cambridge, Massachusetts 02138
(617) 495-4843
http://gseweb.harvard.edu/~ncsall
ncsall@gse.harvard.edu

ISBN 0-8077-4346-1 (paper)

Printed on acid-free paper

Manufactured in the United States of America

11 10 09 08 07 06 05 04   8 7 6 5 4 3 2 1

CONTENTS

 **FOREWORD**

Scientific theories rarely translate directly into classroom practice, and that is proper. Science tries to describe the world as it is; classroom practice tries to alter individuals, in light of certain educational or broader societal goals. We can see this difference dramatically by considering the controversial book about intelligence, *The Bell Curve,* coauthored by Richard Herrnstein and Charles Murray (1994). Readers of the book noted that it was difficult to change intelligence and thus concluded that one should not try. However, in conversation, coauthor Richard Herrnstein admitted that one could draw exactly the opposite conclusion: That is, if it is difficult to change intelligence, one should devote all one's efforts to trying to do so.

In the early 1980s, I developed the theory of multiple intelligences (MI) and described it in *Frames of Mind: The Theory of Multiple Intelligences* (1983). This work was developed as a direct challenge to the standard view of intelligence, as put forth initially by psychologists like Lewis Terman and Charles Spearman, and as articulated most recently by Richard Herrnstein and Charles Murray in the aforementioned book. I argued that all human beings are more accurately described as having a number of relatively autonomous intelligences: At the time, seven, but now it makes sense to recognize at least eight or nine separate intelligences. All human beings possess these intelligences—that is what makes us human, cognitively speaking. But at any moment in time, individuals differ from one another in their profiles of intellectual strengths and weaknesses.

This difference suggests a bridge from science to practice. If humans differ from one another in their profiles of intelligences, educators are faced with a choice. Either we can ignore these differences, and treat all humans as if they simply represent different points on a single bell curve. Or we can take these differences seriously and try, insofar as is possible, to craft an education that addresses each individual in the most appropriate way and also gives each person the opportunity to demonstrate skills and understandings in ways that are comfortable.

I was totally unprepared for the response to these ideas within the world of education. Initially, those concerned with special populations—ranging from children with learning difficulties to those with special talents—showed interest; then interest emerged on the part of those concerned with the education of young children. With the passage of time, other educators and professionals (ranging from museum curators to business people) also became interested in the theory. And most recently, to my surprise and delight, interest in the theory has spread to other countries in other parts of the world. In two subsequent books, *Multiple Intelligences: The Theory in Practice* (1993b) and *Intelligence Reframed: Multiple Intelligences for the 21st Century* (1999), I described some of the ways in which educational practitioners have made use of these ideas in their own teaching, curricular, and assessment innovations.

Until approached by the National Center for the Study of Adult Learning and Literacy, I must admit that I had never thought about uses of MI ideas with adult learners who were trying to master the basic literacies. I saw MI theory as directed primarily to mainstream precollegiate education and as concerned principally with higher order skills in the disciplines, ranging from science and history to art and music. Nonetheless, I was excited to learn that the ideas I had developed might be useful to this underserved population and curious to learn what the team of researchers had discovered.

It has been extremely instructive to follow the course of the AMI Study and now to read its results in the volume that I am introducing. In some ways, I am reminded of the reactions to MI found in typical educational settings: That is, many individuals—teachers as well as students—find the ideas generative and freeing; and many of the pedagogical practices are quite similar to those already used in primary and secondary classrooms around the world.

But I am struck as well by the differences across populations. In particular, some adults who have had difficulty in schooling have developed a certain tentativeness about learning in general, as well as specific attitudes about what it means to be smart and how one should go about learning. They seem to embrace an entity notion of intellect (there is a single thing called smartness and I haven't got it) rather than an incremental view (we can all get smarter, perhaps in several ways) (Dweck & Elliott, 1983). Rather than being stimulated by the unorthodoxy and radicalness of the idea of multiple intelligences, a fair number of them find these ideas unsettling. One almost feels as if they are saying, "Now that I have finally come to school and tried to join the mainstream, you are challenging my ideas about learning and telling me that I should try a new and untested approach to education. I'd better be careful!"

Faced with such a reception, educators have a stark choice. They can either concede the point or revert to "basic skills as usual." In some ways this solution proves the easiest for both students and teachers to adopt. Or they can take this initial wariness as a challenge and attempt to convince their students that it is worth considering different approaches to classroom work and, indeed, a different conception of how the mind works and how one learns.

Happily, most of the teachers in this study have taken this more challenging approach; as reported in these pages, they have probed how initially resistant learners can be aided by an approach that is more individualized and more diversified. It turns out that MI can serve as a "releaser" (helping students to become more assertive, more self-confident) and as a "greaser" (helping them enter smoothly into studies that might have seemed forbidding before). It also turns out that several of the teachers have become deeply interested in research questions—always a happy risk of this kind of university–practitioner partnership.

As several of the authors indicate, such scattered but genuine skepticism raises the question of how best to introduce the ideas and practices of MI. With young children, the idea of multiple intelligences is quite exciting and so there is little reason to hide or sugarcoat it. Indeed, the problem is frequently the reverse: How to keep students (and teachers and parents) from prematurely labeling youngsters as "highly spatial" or "interpersonally challenged." In the case of adult learners who are still acquiring basic skills, it may be more prudent to minimize terms and technology, and simply put into practice promising lessons—"MI-inspired instructions and lessons," to use the terms of the authors.

This study also raises the question of where, in the educational firmament, MI ideas are most likely to be applicable. On the basis of almost two decades of experimentation in school, I had come to believe that MI ideas were most comfortable when specific disciplines (like music or mathematics) were being taught, or when rich concepts (like evolution or democracy) could be conveyed in many symbol systems and analogies. I was somewhat skeptical that MI ideas would prove equally useful with the teaching of foreign languages, or the inculcation of basic skills, like language literacy.

This volume has convinced me that my conservatism was unwarranted. There are a variety of ways in which one theory of the mind—namely, one that recognizes diverse mental faculties—can indeed be drawn on in the teaching of English as a second language or in the dissemination of skills of reading and writing. Indeed, particularly in cases where students may have had a history of difficulty with linguistic and logical spheres, it may be especially important to open up learning to other modes of representation—even when such "opening up" may initially encounter difficulties. It should be said as well that adults have reflective capacities that younger students lack. These reflections about what learning is about and how they themselves best learn can be drawn on to create a far more personalized education for each individual.

Indeed, at the heart of MI theory are educational implications that are precisely the opportunities to create an approach that best suits each group and each individual. We saw this at work years ago in Project Zero's Project Spectrum with preschool children (Gardner, Feldman, & Krechevsky, 1998); and, over the years, the effectiveness of this way of thinking has been brought out in numerous ways in precollegiate education (Kornhaber & Fierros, 2000). Thanks to the pioneering work of Julie Viens, Silja Kallenbach, and AMI teacher–researchers, we now know that, in capable hands, the idea of multiple intelligences has a generative role to play in the education of adults as well.

~Howard Gardner

 **PREFACE**

What Is the Adult Multiple Intelligences (AMI) Study?

The introduction of multiple intelligences theory (MI theory) in 1983 generated considerable interest in the educational community. Multiple intelligences was a provocative new theory, claiming at least seven relatively independent intelligences, in marked contrast to the traditional view of a unitary, "general" intelligence (Gardner, 1983, 1993b). Multiple intelligences theory was intended for an audience of psychologists. Gardner's introduction to MI theory, *Frames of Mind* (1983, 1993a), had little to say about classroom application. Yet many educators who are aware of the many different "smarts" their students bring to the classroom have enthusiastically received it. They are drawn to MI theory because it supports pedagogy and approaches such as whole language, cooperative learning, and multisensory teaching. As a formal theory based on empirical research, it validates what teachers already know and do when they use diverse classroom practices.

The efforts to apply MI theory that have been documented by Gardner and others have been at the pre-K–12, primarily pre-K–8, level. Until late 1996, the adult literacy field had not engaged in a systematic application of MI theory. Adult literacy students, perhaps more than any others, suffered from the consequences of unidimensional views of intelligence, which translated into uniform instructional and assessment approaches that favored logical and linguistic skills. Traditional approaches may have failed to reach and teach many adults when they were children. "Adult literacy" in this Sourcebook refers to a range of educational contexts that includes English for Speakers of Other Languages (ESOL) and Adult Basic Education (ABE) leading to Adult Secondary Education (GED or Adult Diploma).

In light of the positive experiences with MI theory at the pre-K–12 level, together with the promise it holds for the adult literacy field, the AMI Study was conceived. Project Zero and the New England Literacy Resource Center (NELRC)/ World Educa-

tion joined forces to design the AMI Study under the auspices of the National Center for the Study of Adult Learning and Literacy (NCSALL) at Harvard Graduate School of Education.

In December 1996, 10 ESOL, ABE, GED, or diploma preparation teachers from Connecticut, Maine, Massachusetts, Rhode Island, and Vermont embarked on an 18-month journey to understand what the theory of multiple intelligences might have to offer to teaching and learning in their settings. Selected from among 38 applicants to participate in the AMI Study, these teachers took on the challenge to help their students identify and use diverse pathways to learning English, basic skills, and content utilizing MI theory. This Sourcebook represents the culmination of the teachers' AMI research projects.

The study codirectors began the AMI Study by asking, "How can multiple intelligences theory support instruction and assessment in Adult Basic Education (ABE), Adult Secondary Education (ASE), and English for Speakers of Other Languages (ESOL)?" Each teacher developed a research question related to her own practice under the "umbrella" of the overarching question. In addition to keeping a journal of their lessons and reflections, they employed other data collection strategies, such as student observations, interviews, and surveys. The AMI codirectors supported the teachers' research efforts through quarterly institutes, classroom visits, background readings, and online communication. The data from the teacher research projects inform the overall study across the AMI classrooms.

In spring 1999, the AMI Study entered a second phase. Twelve teachers from Baltimore, Houston, Ohio, and Washington (state) were recruited to pilot the first draft of the Sourcebook from April to December 1999. They tried lessons from the Sourcebook, developed or adapted their own MI-based lessons, and reflected on the process in journals and phone meetings. They read and discussed the Sourcebook, chapter by chapter, providing valuable insights and suggestions that informed the revisions and additions made to it.

The AMI teacher research projects are available under one cover from the National Center for the

Study of Adult Learning and Literacy (NCSALL), entitled *Multiple Intelligences in Practice: Teacher Research Reports from the Adult Multiple Intelligences Study.* (See AMI Resources to Download.)

Why Use This Sourcebook?

As a resource meant specifically for practitioners in adult education, *Multiple Intelligences and Adult Literacy* fills a gap in currently available materials about MI theory and its application to teaching and learning. The AMI Study was the first systematic, classroom-based research of MI theory in different adult learning contexts. It provided the opportunity to create this Sourcebook, a resource for teachers starting out using the theory in adult education.

This Sourcebook is an attempt at presenting multiple intelligences—theory, critical issues related to its application, and practical examples—in a way that is appropriate and useful for practitioners in the field. As a group, the AMI team wanted to go beyond the "cookie cutter" or "cookbook" format of many teaching guides. As a research team, we asked ourselves how we would want such a resource organized and formatted, as teachers and "consumers" of the information. The result is a resource designed to facilitate what we have come to believe are the key aspects of applying MI theory: Developing a good understanding of the theory and initiating manageable MI applications for instruction and self-reflection. In other words, we tried to create the resource we wish we had had when starting our own work with MI theory.

The heart of this Sourcebook comes from the AMI teachers and the research projects they carried out in their settings. Rooted firmly in the lived experience of the AMI teachers, this book is an honest look at the successes and challenges involved in using MI theory in adult education.

How This Sourcebook Is Organized

The Sourcebook is organized by important themes and lessons that emerged from the AMI Study. The authors have tried to present what we learned in ways that would be useful as well as thought-provoking. Note that we use the terms "MI-based," "MI-inspired," "MI-informed," and "in the spirit of MI" interchangeably. Throughout this Sourcebook, we tend to equate these terms with nontraditional teaching approaches that go beyond the use of paper, pencil, and blackboard.

The Sourcebook has five chapters, each containing two or more subsections. Each chapter is summarized below.

Chapter 1: MI Basics

An important aspect of applying MI theory is knowing the theory well. This chapter covers the basics of MI theory and its major tenets. Although there is no single "right" way to apply the theory, there are those applications that are more (or less) "in the spirit" of MI theory, that is, applications that use MI theory's major tenets as guides and do not contradict its main suppositions. For example, any application of MI theory should acknowledge in some way the plurality of intelligences. With a deeper understanding of the theory comes a better sense of how best to use it in practice.

Chapter 2: MI Reflections

Most teachers who start using MI theory eventually have to consider whether they will present the theory to their students explicitly or keep it implicitly woven into the curriculum. This chapter focuses on teaching about MI theory and using it as a tool for student reflection and self-understanding. The first section summarizes the AMI teachers' goals, practices, and other issues central to MI Reflections. The two middle sections offer perspectives on MI Reflections from AMI teachers. The last section of this chapter presents an array of lesson ideas for exploring MI theory with students. We hope this chapter is helpful to practitioners who are deciding whether or how to teach about MI theory.

Chapter 3: MI-inspired Instruction

The authors often refer to MI theory as a lens through which we can view and understand our students and our approaches to teaching and learning. The AMI Study experience confirms the notion that there is no one way to apply MI theory in instruction. Depending on the teaching context and goals, as well as each teacher's own "take" on MI theory, a tremendous variety of MI-informed practices have emerged. At the same time, the AMI Study has identified several common features of MI-informed teaching and learning in adult learning settings. The first section of this chapter presents these common features, whereas the second section presents the experiences and points of view of two AMI teachers.

Chapter 4: MI-inspired Lessons

The lessons presented in this chapter are concrete examples of how the AMI teachers translated MI theory to their own settings. Only lessons that were implemented by one or more teachers were chosen for this collection. The first section offers ideas for different MI-based lesson formats. Subjects commonly taught in ABE, GED, and ESOL classes organize the sections that follow. Teachers are encouraged to use and modify these lessons. We hope that they serve as an inspiring and useful starting point for teachers to develop their own MI-based lessons, assessments, and projects.

Chapter 5: Student Responses to MI Practices

The first section of this chapter details the AMI Study's findings about student responses to the MI practices students experienced. With this chapter, we hope to prepare teachers for likely student responses. We share our insights regarding how to apply MI in ways that will help students see its relevance to their lives and studies.

How to Use This Sourcebook

There is an argument to be made for starting your reading of the Sourcebook with Chapter 1. Reading this introduction to the basics of MI first will help you form a basic theoretical understanding of multiple intelligences and will set the stage for developing MI-based practices in your setting. The theory should serve as a touch point against which to check emerging MI practices.

The order in which subsequent chapters are read is not vital. It might be useful to skim through and choose those pieces that are of most interest and seem most relevant to you. Also, there is some overlap across sections of the Sourcebook. This overlap is complementary, not redundant, information related to different themes and ideas that emerge in the application of MI theory. To make finding connections across sections easier, we have included cross-referencing throughout the Sourcebook.

We encourage readers, if at all possible, to work with a buddy or team and use formats such as study circles. The AMI teachers found the opportunities to discuss their evolving understanding and practices related to MI with colleagues valuable as they learned about and applied MI theory. The AMI Sourcebook pilot teachers stressed the value of rereading the Sourcebook after you have tried MI-based approaches.

Statement of Goals

We hope this Sourcebook will help readers attain these four basic goals:

1. Develop or enhance a basic understanding of MI theory and how it can be applied in adult literacy (ABE, GED, ESOL) education.

2. Develop an understanding of the promises and challenges related to using MI theory as a tool for self-reflection and self-understanding.

3. Learn how multiple intelligences theory can be used to develop learning experiences, MI-inspired instructional strategies, that tap students' intelligence strengths.

4. Determine an appropriate path for using MI theory in one's own teaching context.

 # ACKNOWLEDGMENTS

All of us who have worked on the AMI Study would like to thank our families and loved ones for their support and understanding during the often demanding AMI work. We acknowledge our indebtedness to Dr. Howard Gardner whose theory and writings informed and inspired this project. We are grateful for the advice and assistance we received from Drs. Heidi Andrade, Susan Baum, John Comings, Ellie Drago-Severson, Susan Lytle, and Bruce Torff. We thank our interns, Deborah Anderson, Gina Cobin, Lori Eisenberg, Katty Fernandez, Marina Livis, and Kofi-Charu Nat Turner.

The AMI Pilot Teachers

The Sourcebook was improved exponentially by the efforts of the AMI pilot teachers. This dedicated group piloted the Sourcebook for the better part of 1999. Their insights and experiences have found a home throughout these pages, and we thank them for their inspired participation and invaluable contributions.

Carol Beima
Adult Education Program
Clark College
Vancouver, WA

Ronald Butler
Carl Ripken Learning Center
Baltimore READS
Baltimore, MD

Stella Edwards
ABLE Program
Dayton Public Schools
Dayton, OH

Edmund Carter Frost
Adult Education and Literacy Houston Community
College System
Houston, TX

Judy Hickey
The Learning Bank
Baltimore, MD

Robert Hofmann
Adult Education Program
Community Correctional Center
Lebanon, OH

William Kepp
Oregon Career and Technology Center
Oregon, OH

Rebecca Martin
Bayland Learning Center
Houston READ Commission
Houston, TX

Lynn Pinder
The Learning Bank
Baltimore, MD

Helen Sablan
Adult Education Program
Tacoma Community College
Tacoma, WA

Jan Tucker
Families That Work
Edmonds Community College
Lynnwood, WA

Jean Voelkel
Adult Education Program
Community Correctional Center
Lebanon, OH

AMI Advisory Council

The AMI Study has also benefited from the insights and assistance of a nine-member advisory council. We appreciate the range of expertise and viewpoints of the advisors. The advisors and their affiliations at the time were as follows:

Elsa Auerbach
Associate Professor
English Department
University of Massachusetts
Boston, MA

Evelyn Beaulieu
Director
Center for Adult Learning and Literacy
University of Maine
Orono, ME

Don Chao and Kathy Hanaway
Staff Development Specialists
Adult Training and Development Network, CT

Janet Isserlis
Director
Rhode Island Literacy Resources
Brown University
Providence, RI

Martha Merson
Adult Basic Education/Literacy Specialist
Adult Literacy Resource Institute
Boston, MA

Andy Nash
Equipped for the Future
Staff Development Specialist
New England Literacy Resource Center/
World Education
Boston, MA

Dorothy Oliver
Staff Development Specialist
NH Department of Education
Concord, NH

Mary Jane Schmitt
Math Staff Development Specialist
Harvard Graduate School of Education
Cambridge, MA

Alison Simmons
Staff Development Specialist
SABES/ World Education
Boston, MA

We also appreciate the feedback and suggestions we received from many additional people nationwide on the draft version of this Sourcebook.

Chapter 1: MI BASICS

Introduction

It's early evening in Salisbury, Massachusetts, and the GED preparation class is in full swing. Working alone or in pairs, the students use rulers, Play-Doh®, drawing materials, measuring spoons, even a xylophone, to complete three measuring tasks of their choosing from the 10 diverse options Martha Jean, their teacher, has provided. One student measures and cuts strips of paper; another measures her partner's height, while a pair measures and compares differing amounts of water and Play-Doh®. Lively discussions about inches, gallons, and long and short musical notes create a welcomed din to Martha's ears.

In Providence, Rhode Island, Terri Coustan's low literacy ESOL students are completing entries in their dialogue journals. Because her students had responded enthusiastically to visual media in the past, Terri has begun including in the journals photographs of each student at work in the classroom. The journals are an important part of Terri's attempts to help her students reflect on their own learning. Watching her students so engaged with the photos and intently writing journal responses, Terri is encouraged. She feels she has found one strategy to help circumvent the significant language barrier that has obstructed her previous attempts at guiding her students' self-reflection.

Not far from Terri's classroom, at Providence's Dorcas Place, Lezlie Rocka teaches a basic literacy class. One student stands and reads dramatically from a book. Later, students trace the travels of Sojourner Truth, the book's main character, on individual maps. At another point, they sketch pictures of a scene as they imagine it. Lezlie has devised several diverse hands-on activities, tied to the plot and theme of the readings, that she intermingles with student readings. For Lezlie, these activities help build her students' reading comprehension. For the students, it is fun and an engaging way to learn to read.

Which of these teachers is using multiple intelligences (MI) theory to inform her practice? All three, as the reader has likely guessed. But if that's the case, then why are these MI-informed practices so different from one another? MI theory is a theory of intelligence, not a specific approach or set of teaching strategies merely to be replicated. MI theory serves as a *common theoretical root* that results in many *different practical applications* across many different learning contexts.

The teacher–researchers of the Adult Multiple Intelligences (AMI) Study, including the teachers introduced in our vignettes above, used MI theory in different ways to design applications to address their own goals and circumstances. With MI theory at their root, the diverse practices that emerged across the AMI sites still shared many commonalities.

Whatever the practical outcome, the AMI teachers, like many teachers before and after them, began with the basics, asking, "What is the theory of multiple intelligences? What are the major features of MI theory with implications for the classroom? What are those implications of MI theory?" Beginning with these initial queries, the AMI teachers tried first to understand MI theory well, in order to develop appropriate applications that fit their needs and remained consonant with MI theory.

The goal of this chapter is to provide those "basics" of MI theory: what it is and in what ways it can inform practice. The chapter is organized in two parts: the theoretical basics and practical basics. The theoretical basics include MI theory versus traditional definitions of intelligence, a description of each intelligence, the criteria used to identify intelligences, and features of MI theory with direct implications for the classroom. The theory basics are followed by an overview of how MI theory is put into practice, highlighting examples from the AMI classrooms. Final Reflection and Discussion Questions at the end of the chapter are meant both to help readers check their understanding of MI theory and to consider how they might tap into MI theory in their own setting.

Multiple Intelligences: The Theory Behind the Practice[*]

The Traditional View

The traditional view of intelligence can be traced to French psychologist Alfred Binet. At the request of the French Ministry of Education in the early 1900s, Binet and his colleague Theodore Simon developed a test that identified children at risk for school failure. The test was effective for that purpose. However, it was soon used as the basis for "measuring" individuals' general intelligence. Since that time, intelligence tests have been heavily weighted with the types of highly predictive abilities Binet measured in his test, such as verbal memory and reasoning, numerical reasoning, and appreciation of logical sequences.

In 1912, German psychologist Wilhelm Stern came up with the Intelligence Quotient, or IQ, which represents the ratio of one's "mental age" to one's chronological age, as measured by intelligence tests. Lewis Terman, an American psychometrician, is credited (or blamed) for popularizing the IQ test in the United States starting in the 1920s. Terman introduced the Stanford-Binet IQ tests, the first paper-and-pencil, group-administered versions of the test.

In large part as a result of Terman's work, the intelligence test quickly became a standard part of the U.S. educational landscape. Since that time, conventional wisdom has equated intelligence with this psychometric view. Terman's work also had a significant role in the development of two additional beliefs about intelligence: that it is inherited and largely unchangeable. Current conventional wisdom about intelligence includes three main dimensions: Intelligence is measured by a test; we inherit our intelligence from our parents and are

born with whatever intelligence we will ever possess; and because intelligence is one general capacity, we can all be measured against the same yardstick, plotted on a single line somewhere between "very stupid" and "highly gifted."

In recent years IQ tests have gradually seen less use. Legal battles have made public schools back away from them. For the most part IQ testing is limited to cases where there is a problem, like a suspected learning disability, or where selection procedures apply, like entry into a gifted program. However, the line of thinking to which intelligence testing gave rise maintains a powerful presence. Most directly, many academic measures are thinly disguised intelligence tests. Most pervasively, the traditional view of intelligence, internalized on a societal level, plays a major role in shaping our educational policies and practices. The traditional view of intelligence has played a significant role in determining standard school fare, with its emphasis on the same narrow set of language and math skills that revert to test items. "Core curricula" as well as determinants of who are the "good" or "smart" students find their roots in this long-held view of intelligence.

A New View

Howard Gardner was certainly not the first to take issue with IQ tests and the concept of intelligence that they support. Criticisms emerged from the inception of intelligence testing, particularly when IQ tests first hit the U.S. educational scene in the 1920s. The influential American journalist Walter Lippman took Lewis Terman to task in a series of debates that were published in the *New Republic*. He criticized the superficiality of the test items and the risks of assessing intellectual potential through a single, brief method, and he pointed out possible cultural biases. However, nothing really changed. As Gardner (199b) notes,

> So long as these tests continued to do what they were supposed to do—that is, yield reasonable predictions about people's success in school—it did not seem necessary or prudent to probe too deeply into their meanings or to explore alternative views of what intelligence is or how it might be assessed. (p. 13)

It is in his own work in neuropsychology and cognitive development that Gardner began to question the traditional view of intelligence. In the 1970s and 1980s he worked in two contexts studying the

---

[*] Much of the text for this section, "Multiple Intelligences: The Theory Behind the Practice," draws from Gardner (1999), *Intelligences Reframed*.

nature of human cognitive capacities. At the Boston University Aphasia Research Center, Gardner conducted studies to understand the patterns of abilities of stroke victims suffering from impaired language and other kinds of cognitive and emotional injury. At the same time, he worked with ordinary and gifted children at Project Zero, at the Harvard Graduate School of Education, in an attempt to understand the development of cognitive abilities. Gardner (1999) observed something different, not explained by the psychometric view of intelligence. He noted,

> The daily opportunity to work with children and with brain-damaged adults impressed me with one brute fact of human nature: People have a wide range of capacities. A person's strength in one area of performance simply does not predict any comparable strength in other areas.
>
> In most cases, however, strengths are distributed in a skewed fashion. For instance, a person may be skilled in acquiring foreign languages, yet be unable to find her way around an unfamiliar environment or learn a new song or figure out who occupies a position of power in a crowd of strangers. Likewise, weakness in learning foreign languages does not predict either success or failure with most other cognitive tasks. (p. 31)

Both groups with which he worked sent Gardner the same message:

> The human mind is better thought of as a series of relatively separate faculties, with only loose and non-predictable relations with one another, than a single, all-purpose machine that performs steadily at a certain horsepower, independent of content and context. (p. 32)

Most theories of intelligence looked only at problem-solving and ignored the creation of products. They also assumed that their notion of "intelligence" would be apparent and appreciated anywhere, regardless of cultural values and beliefs. In this respect, Gardner (1999) distinguished his theory of intelligence from others by defining intelligence as "the ability to solve problems or to create products that are valued within one or more cultural settings" (p. 33).

Gardner (1999) recently refined his definition of intelligence:

> Intelligence [is] a biopsychological potential to process information that can be activated in a cultural setting to solve problems or create products that are of value in a culture. (pp. 33–34)

His revised definition suggests that intelligence represents *potential* that may or may not be realized depending on the values, available opportunities, and personal decisions made by individuals of a particular culture.

Gardner's definition locates intelligence in what people can do and the products they create in the real world, in contrast to intelligence implied by a test score. It suggests a qualitative expression, a description, of an individual's collection of intelligences rather than a quantitative expression of a general ability.

The Eight Intelligences

At present eight intelligences—eight qualitatively independent ways to be intelligent—have been identified. Each intelligence is relatively distinct neurologically as well as in the symbol system it uses, the subabilities included in each, and how each is used in the real world. In the pages that follow, each of the intelligences is described according to several categories defined in Figure 1.1.

Figure 1.1. Key to Intelligence Descriptions

Key abilities are broad abilities central to that intelligence.

Subabilities are the more specific abilities within each of the intelligences.

Roles or **Domains** refer to societal niches that emphasize that particular intelligence. For example, the journalist role requires a great deal of linguistic intelligence. Domains refer to the disciplines of the real world, activities that are valued and at which we can get better. The domains listed for each intelligence require a great deal of that intelligence. (Roles are played within domains.)

Strategies or **Products** refer to ways of learning or engaging in a task associated with that intelligence, or the products that emerge from work that emphasizes that particular intelligence. Interviewing is a strategy and an article is a product of a journalist who is to a great degree relying on his linguistic intelligence.

Everyday Uses: As our intellectual toolkit, we use our multiple intelligences in combination for everyday activities. This category describes everyday contexts in which the intelligence is heavily drawn on.

"NOT" refers to common misconceptions about the nature of that intelligence. For example, liking to talk does not imply a high level of linguistic intelligence.

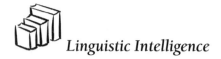 *Linguistic Intelligence*

> Linguistic intelligence is the capacity to use language, your native language, and perhaps other languages, to express what's on your mind and to understand other people. Poets really specialize in linguistic intelligence, but any kind of writer, orator, speaker, lawyer, or a person for whom language is an important stock in trade, highlights linguistic intelligences.
>
> ~ Howard Gardner (Gardner & Checkley, 1997, p. 12)

Key Abilities of Linguistic Intelligence
...involves perceiving or generating spoken or written language.
...allows communication and sense making through language.
...includes sensitivity to subtle meanings in language.

Subabilities
expressive language, invented narrative/storytelling
descriptive/instructional language, reporting
poetic use of language, wordplay

Roles or Domains that require significant linguistic intelligence

novelist	stand-up comedian	law
journalist	preacher	coaching
poet	dispatcher	teaching

Strategies or Products that emphasize linguistic intelligence

instructions/manuals	script	word game
novel	newspaper	discussion
debate/speech	play	lyrics/libretto

Everyday uses of linguistic intelligence
reading the newspaper
writing a letter
participating in a meeting

Linguistic Intelligence is NOT
...bilingualism (but might include facility with learning languages).
...being talkative, liking to talk.

Logical-Mathematical Intelligence

> People with highly developed logical-mathematical intelligence understand the underlying principles of some kind of a causal system, the way a scientist or a logician does; or can manipulate numbers, quantities, and operations, the way a mathematician does.

> ~ Howard Gardner (Gardner & Checkley, 1997, p. 12)

Key Abilities of Logical-Mathematical Intelligence
...enables individuals to use and appreciate abstract relations.
...includes facility in the use of numbers and logical thinking.

Subabilities
numerical reasoning (calculations, estimation, quantification)
logical problem-solving (focusing on overall structure and relationships, making logical inferences)

Roles or Domains that require significant logical-mathematical intelligence

math teacher	scientist	engineering
architect	computer programmer	building
budget analyst	accountant	knitting

Strategies or Products that emphasize logical-mathematical intelligence

graph	spread sheet	flow chart
timeline	equations/mathematical proof	invention
computer program	business plan	logic puzzle

Everyday uses of logical-mathematical intelligence
reading the bus schedule
solving puzzles
managing family checkbook

Logical-mathematical ability is NOT
...only oriented to numbers (and includes nonnumerical logical relations).

Musical Intelligence

Musical intelligence is the capacity to think in music, to be able to hear patterns, recognize them, remember them, and perhaps manipulate them. People who have a strong musical intelligence don't just remember music easily—they can't get it out of their minds, it's so omnipresent. Now, some people will say, "Yes, music is important, but it's a talent, not an intelligence." And I say, "Fine, let's call it a talent." But, then we have to leave the word intelligent out of all discussions of human abilities. You know, Mozart was damned smart!

~ Howard Gardner (Gardner & Checkley, 1997, p. 12)

Key Abilities of Musical Intelligence
...involves perceiving and understanding patterns of sound.
...includes creating and communicating meaning from sound.

Subabilities
    musical perception
    musical production
    musical composition/notation

Roles or Domains that require significant musical intelligence
    musician   choreographer   music critic
    conductor   disc jockey   piano tuner
    composer   sound engineer   cheerleader

Strategies or Products that emphasize musical intelligence
    composition/song   critique/analysis   jingle
    recital/performance ·   sound effects   musical/opera
    dance set to music   soundtrack/accompaniment   recording/sampling

Everyday uses of musical intelligence
    appreciating a song on the radio
    singing in a choir
    playing a musical instrument
    distinguishing different sounds of the car

Musical intelligence is NOT
    ...engaged by playing "background" music.

 *Spatial Intelligence*

Spatial intelligence refers to the ability to represent the spatial world internally—the way a sailor or airplane pilot navigates the large spatial world, or the way a chess player or sculptor represents a more circumscribed spatial world. Spatial intelligence can be used in the arts or in the sciences. If you are spatially intelligent and oriented toward the arts, you are more likely to become a painter or a sculptor or an architect than, say, a musician or a writer. Similarly, certain sciences like anatomy or topology emphasize spatial intelligence.

~ Howard Gardner (Gardner & Checkley, 1997, p. 12)

Key Abilities of Spatial Intelligence
...involves perceiving and transforming visual or 3-D information.
...allows for the re-creation of images from memory.

Subabilities
understanding causal or functional relationships through observation
use of spatial information to navigate through space
sensitive perception or observation of visual world and arts
production of visual information or works of art

Roles or Domains that require significant spatial intelligence

gardener	sculptor	surgeon
mechanic	house painter	carpenter
photographer	dancer	athlete

Strategies or Products that emphasize spatial intelligence

graph/chart	painting	blueprints
diagram	film, TV program	map
sculpture	model	invention

Everyday uses of spatial intelligence
finding one's way in an unfamiliar town
giving/using directions
playing chess/checkers

Spatial intelligence is NOT
...necessarily visual (note that blind people gain excellent spatial abilities).

Bodily-Kinesthetic Intelligence

Bodily-kinesthetic intelligence is the capacity to use your whole body or parts of your body—your hand, your fingers, your arms—to solve a problem, make something, or put on some kind of a production. The most evident examples are people in athletics or the performing arts, particularly dance or acting.

~ Howard Gardner (Gardner & Checkley, 1997, p. 12)

Key Abilities of Bodily-Kinesthetic Intelligence
...allows an individual to use one's body to create products or solve problems.
...refers to the ability to control all or isolated parts of one's body.

Subabilities
athletic movement
creative movement (including responsiveness to music)
body control and fine motor abilities
generating movement ideas (such as in choreography)

Roles or Domains that require significant bodily-kinesthetic intelligence

dancer	athlete	actor
coach	artisan	mime
sculptor	sign language interpreter	surgeon

Strategies or Products that emphasize bodily-kinesthetic intelligence

dance performance	mime	performance art
play	weaving	painting or other
sports/games	jewelry	art product

Everyday uses of bodily-kinesthetic intelligence
playing on a softball team
standing and staying balanced in a moving subway car
riding a bike
fixing something delicate

Bodily-kinesthetic intelligence is NOT
...necessarily demonstrated by an "antsy" or physically active child.
...unstructured release of "energy" through physical activity.

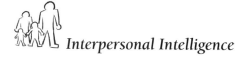 *Interpersonal Intelligence*

> Interpersonal intelligence is understanding other people. It's an ability we all need, but is at a premium if you are a teacher, clinician, salesperson, or politician. Anybody who deals with other people has to be skilled in the interpersonal sphere.
>
> ~ Howard Gardner (Gardner & Checkley, 1997, p. 12)

Key Abilities of Interpersonal Intelligence
...is a sensitivity to the feelings, beliefs, moods, and intentions of other people.
...involves the use of that understanding to work effectively with others.
...includes capitalizing on interpersonal skills in pursuit of one's own ends.

Subabilities
assumption of distinctive social roles (e.g., leader, friend, caregiver)
ability to reflect analytically on the social environment, others
taking action (e.g., political activist, counselor, educator)

Roles or Domains that require significant interpersonal intelligence
educator	counselor	diplomat
activist	social scientist/researcher	religious leader
community organizer	management consultant	negotiator/arbitrator

Strategies or Products that emphasize interpersonal intelligence
tutoring/teaching	democratic classroom	community action
moral dilemmas	action research	peer mediation
play	leadership opportunities	community service

Everyday uses of interpersonal intelligence
retail transactions
asking or giving directions
interactions with coworkers
parenting

Interpersonal intelligence is NOT
...a preference for working in a group.
...being well-liked.
...being polite, possessing the "social graces."
...being ethical or humane.

Intrapersonal Intelligence

Intrapersonal intelligence refers to having an understanding of yourself, of knowing who you are, what you can do, what you want to do, how you react to things, which things to avoid, and which things to gravitate toward. We are drawn to people who have a good understanding of themselves because those people tend not to screw up. They tend to know what they can do. They tend to know what they can't do. And they tend to know where to go if they need help.

~ Howard Gardner (Gardner & Checkley, 1997, p. 12)

Key Abilities of Intrapersonal Intelligence
...enables individuals to have self-knowledge.
...involves using self-knowledge to make decisions.
...includes the ability to distinguish one's feelings, moods, and intentions and to anticipate one's reactions to future courses of action.

Subabilities
self-understanding, the ability to self-reflect analytically
articulating that understanding through other types of expression/ intelligences (poetry, painting, song, and so on)
using that self-knowledge well, toward personal or community goals

Roles or Domains that require significant intrapersonal intelligence
therapist	poet	motivational speaker
psychologist	artist	activist
musician	spiritual/religious leader	philosopher

Strategies or Products that emphasize intrapersonal intelligence
family tree	portfolio/reflections	sermon
poem	journal/diary	action plan
artwork	musical composition/lyrics	autobiography

Everyday uses of intrapersonal intelligence
job/career assessment
religious practices
therapy

Intrapersonal intelligence is NOT
...preferring to work alone and/or in isolation.

Naturalist Intelligence

Naturalist intelligence designates the human ability to discriminate among living things (plants, animals) as well as sensitivity to other features of the natural world (clouds, rock configurations). This ability was clearly of value in our evolutionary past as hunters, gatherers, and farmers; it continues to be central in such roles as botanist or chef. I also speculate that much of our consumer society exploits the naturalist intelligences, which can be mobilized in the discrimination among cars, sneakers, kinds of makeup, and the like.

~ Howard Gardner (Gardner & Checkley, 1997, p. 12).

Key Abilities of Naturalist Intelligence
...is the ability to understand the natural world well and to work in it effectively.
...allows us to distinguish among, classify, and use features of the environment.
...is also applied to nonnatural classifying and patterning.

Subabilities
observational skills
pattern recognition and classification
employing knowledge of the natural world to solve problems

Roles or Domains that require significant naturalist intelligence

florist	fisherman	chef
botanist	environmental educator	farming
biologist	forest ranger	sailing

Strategies or Products that emphasize naturalist intelligence

plants/flowers	surveys of flora/fauna	field notes
animal husbandry	studies/experiments	nature walks
"Outward Bound"	creating and using classification systems	

Everyday uses of naturalist intelligence
cooking
gardening
organizing CDs or other collection

Naturalist intelligence is NOT
...limited to the outside world.

Identifying Intelligences

If there are qualitatively different ways to be intelligent, then how does one identify and characterize each of these separate abilities? In his investigation Gardner looked at the many abilities human beings possess and the diverse roles we play, and he asked what might be the basic biological faculties responsible for these abilities that we observe every day.

To determine these faculties, or "intelligences," Gardner turned to several different areas of study across disciplines, including cognitive psychology, brain research, human development, evolutionary theory and history, cross-cultural comparisons, and the arts and humanities. Gardner's work gave rise to a list of eight criteria he and his colleagues used to identify whether an ability should be designated as a basic human intelligence. These criteria are described in more detail below.

Drawing from different disciplines, several of the criteria provide different ways to tease apart a particular candidate intelligence from other abilities. The idea is that if we can consistently isolate a particular ability in different disciplines and tasks, then that is strong evidence as to its designation as an intelligence—a basic human ability. For example, linguistic intelligence can be isolated: In the brain, as stroke victims lose or preserve language ability apart from other abilities; among special populations, where individuals demonstrate high levels of linguistic ability alone, and developmentally, in that a developmental path for language has been identified.

Some criteria emphasize the universality of a particular ability; for example, evidence of music has been found in all known cultures. Other criteria represent the societal and cultural value placed on particular abilities, for example, identifying abilities for which human beings have developed symbol systems, like language, music, and math.

The Eight Criteria Used to Identify Intelligences

1. *Potential Isolation by Brain Damage/ Neurological Evidence*

This criterion calls for evidence that one intelligence can be isolated from others at the neuro-logical or brain level. The extent to which a specific ability is destroyed or spared as a result of brain damage, such as with stroke patients, tells us about the character of our most basic faculties. In Gardner's (1999) words,

> Every stroke represents an accident of nature from which the careful observer can learn much. Suppose, for example, one wants to study the relation between the ability to speak fluently and the ability to sing fluently. One can mount arguments indefinitely about the relatedness or the independence of these faculties, but the facts of brain damage actually resolve the debate. Human singing and human language are different faculties, that can be independently damaged or spared. Paradoxically, however, human *signing* and human speaking are similar faculties. Those parts of the brain that subserve spoken language in hearing people are (roughly speaking) the same parts of the brain that subserve sign language in deaf people. So here we encounter an underlying linguistic faculty that cuts across sensory and motor modalities. (p. 30, emphasis in original)

The existence of a separate musical intelligence is strongly suggested by cases of brain injury in which musical ability is preserved, but other abilities, such as language, are lost. In other words, musical ability has been isolated in the brain. Other findings, such as the identification of brain centers for linguistic and musical processing, provide more neurological evidence that these and other abilities are basic human abilities, or intelligences. For example, specific areas of the brain have been identified as playing important roles in music perception and production, suggesting a separate musical intelligence.

2. *Evolutionary History and Evolutionary Plausibility*

Evidence from evolutionary science is central to any understanding of human cognition or intelligence. For example, we see evidence in early human beings of a naturalist intelligence, that is, the understanding and use of flora and fauna. The existence of an intelligence is also suggested when evolutionary evidence of it is found in other species, for example, highly developed spatial capacities in other mammals. Evolutionary evidence for musical intelligence is drawn from its central role in Stone Age societies and its link to other species, as in the case of birdsong.

3. *An Identifiable Set of Core Operation(s)*

Although intelligences operate in rich contexts, usually in combination with other intelligences, it is helpful to isolate abilities that seem central to an intelligence. For example, linguistic intelligence includes the following core operations: distinguishing meaningful sounds (phonemic discrimination), a command of grammar and sentence structure (syntax), a sensitivity to the practical uses of language (pragmatics), and acquisition of word meanings (semantics). The core operations of spatial intelligence include sensitivity to large-scale, local, three- and two-dimensional spaces, whereas the core operations that trigger musical ability include sensitivity to pitch, rhythm, and timbre. The existence of specified core operations for an ability contributes to its identification as an intelligence.

4. *Susceptibility to Encoding in a Symbol System*

Human beings spend a great deal of time learning and using different kinds of symbol systems. Our primary communications occur through symbol systems like written and spoken language, mathematical systems such as logical equations, and picturing (e.g., charts and graphs). Over time people developed these symbol systems to communicate information in an organized and accurate manner. Indeed, symbol systems seem to have arisen to code those meanings to which human intelligences are most sensitive. Therefore, a fundamental criterion of an intelligence is its embodiment in a symbol system. Musical notation is another example of a distinct symbol system.

5. *Distinctive Developmental Path*

Intelligences are not demonstrated "in the raw." Rather, they operate in different domains and in combination with one another. For example, musical intelligence is expressed in many domains and adult roles, including musician, composer, and sound engineer. Within any given domain, intelli-

gences have their own developmental histories. Both the musician and the sound engineer will develop their musical intelligence, but along the developmental path needed for their respective roles. An individual who wants to be a softball player must develop his or her abilities in ways distinct from those of the aspiring dancer. Other people follow distinctive developmental paths to develop the interpersonal intelligence to become, for instance, clinicians or clergymen. The developmental paths within domains help us to identify the abilities, or intelligences, at their root across domains.

It is important to assume a cross-cultural perspective, because an intelligence may be brought to bear in cultures that exhibit quite different roles and values. For example, both the clinician in American culture and the shaman in a tribal culture are using their interpersonal intelligences, but in different ways and for somewhat different ends (Gardner, 1999).

6. *Existence of Savants, Prodigies, and Other Individuals Distinguished by the Presence or Absence of Specific Abilities*

Individuals who have unusual profiles of intelligence offer another area to explore in identifying intelligences. These profiles often include high-level ability in an isolated area of ability, suggesting that that particular ability may be an intelligence.

Savants, prodigies, and autistic individuals exhibit a high level of ability in one area while other abilities are typically ordinary or severely impaired. Many autistic children, for example, possess outstanding abilities in areas like calculations, musical performance, and drawing. At the same time, they demonstrate severe impairments in communication, language, and sensitivity to others.

As with autism, prodigious ability tends to show up in domains that are rule-governed and that require little life experience, such as chess, mathematics, representational drawing, and other forms of pattern recognition and reproduction. The specific, isolated abilities among these groups provide evidence as to which abilities should be considered intelligences, that is, those that have biological bases and operate relatively independently (Gardner, 1999).

7. *Support From Experimental Psychological Tasks*

We should also be able to use experimental psychological tasks to isolate intelligences. For example, task interference can help us to identify discrete intelligences. In studies of task interference, researchers study the extent to which two actions are related to each other by observing how well—or poorly—individuals carry out both simultaneously. If doing one activity does not interfere with the successful completion of the other, then we can assume that the activities draw on different abilities. For example, most individuals are able to walk while they talk. The intelligences most involved in walking (bodily-kinesthetic, spatial) and having a discussion (linguistic, interpersonal) work separately from one another. And yet most people find it hard to hold a conversation when working on another highly linguistic activity, like doing a crossword puzzle or listening to a song with lyrics. Being able to separate out a certain type of ability experimentally provides strong support for that ability as an intelligence.

8. *Support From Psychometric Findings*

A high correlation between certain subtests on standardized tests suggests a single intelligence at work in both subtests, whereas a low correlation suggests separate intelligences are at work. Therefore, one can say that much current psychometric evidence is a criticism of MI theory, given that the high correlation in scores among various tasks suggests a general or unitary intelligence.

However, as psychologists have broadened their definitions of intelligence and added to their tools for measurement, psychometric evidence has emerged favoring MI theory. For example, more recent studies of spatial and linguistic intelligences strongly suggest that these two areas are relatively separate, having at best only a weak correlation when tested. Similar measures of musical acuity can be teased apart from other tasks, supporting the identification of a separate musical intelligence. Research on social intelligence (inter- and intrapersonal intelligences) suggests abilities that are different from standard linguistic and logical intelligences (Rosnow, Skedler, Jaeger, & Rind, 1994).

The Criteria in Conclusion

With varying amounts and quality of research on the different candidate abilities, Gardner and his colleagues asked whether an ability met the set of criteria reasonably well. If it did, it was designated an intelligence. If the ability did not meet the criteria reasonably well, then it might be set aside, or recast and reinvestigated against the criteria. Naturalist intelligence was added in 1995, 12 years after the initial presentation of MI theory, which featured seven intelligences, but soon after sufficient brain evidence emerged.

An existential intelligence is under consideration by Gardner and his colleagues. Existential ability refers to the human inclination to ask very basic questions about existence (Who are we? Where do we come from? Is there a God?) and finds a home in mythology and philosophy. However, it has not sufficiently fulfilled the criteria. In particular, neurological evidence has not been established. The question remains as to whether existential abilities are not an amalgam of logical and linguistic intelligences (Gardner, 1999).

The criteria have served well as the principal means to identify a set of intelligences that captures a reasonably complete range of abilities valued by human cultures. By keeping the criteria in active use, MI theory can and has been modified to reflect our increasing understanding of the ways in which people are intelligent. Using the criteria to identify our basic human intelligences, MI theory offers the most accurate description to date of intelligence in the real world, and it continues to be a helpful articulation and organization of human abilities.

Figure 1.2. Distinguishing Features of MI Theory

- Definition of intelligence based on real world intelligence

- Pluralistic view of intelligence

- All eight (or more) intelligences are universal

- Unique profiles of intelligence that develop and change

- Each intelligence involves subabilities or different manifestations

- Intelligences work in combination in domains, not isolation

Key Features of MI Theory

At least six distinguishing features of MI theory have particular implications for educational practice (Figure 1.2). Each is presented in this section.

A Definition of Intelligence Based on Real World Intelligence

MI theory's definition of intelligence sets it apart from the conventional understanding of intelligence: "Intelligence [is] a biopsychological potential to process information that can be activated in a cultural setting to solve problems or create products that are of value in a culture" (Gardner, 1999, pp. 33–34). MI theory's definition of intelligence locates intelligence in real world problem-solving and product making and accounts for the cultural dimension of what counts as intelligence. In contrast to the "implied" view of intelligence of IQ tests, MI theory is based on an understanding of how people's intelligences really operate.

A Pluralistic View of Intelligence

The second feature is that there exists a plurality of intelligences, each with its own symbol system and ways of knowing and processing information. This is in distinct contrast to the traditional view of intelligence, which asserts the existence of one general intelligence that is put to use to solve any problem, no matter what the task or domain. Using the criteria (see above), eight distinct intelligences have been identified.

All Eight (or more) Intelligences Are Universal

MI theory holds that intelligence originates biologically; that is, all human beings are at promise for each of the intelligences. All the intelligences have been identified across all known cultures/societies. This propensity for the intelligences might indeed be considered a significant contributor to what makes us human.

Unique Profiles of Intelligence That Develop and Change

Although MI theory claims a biological basis of intelligence, this does not suggest that intelligence is purely genetic and inherited. Nature suggests we are all at promise for all the intelligences. How and to what extent the intelligences manifest themselves depend on "nurture" to a significant degree.

An individual's intelligences develop and change; intelligence is not solely inherited and develops based on interaction with our environment. Cultural, societal, and individual factors shape how much we see of a particular intelligence and how it is manifested. For example, in the case of linguistic intelligence, writing might dominate in one context and storytelling in another. A child in the first context, where the written word is emphasized at school and home, who has access to a computer, books, and writing implements might develop his or her linguistic ability in the area of writing. A child in a culture with a strong oral tradition might develop his or her oral linguistic intelligence in the area of storytelling or preaching. Whatever the specific nature of the intelligence, the more time an individual spends using an intelligence, and the more accessible and better the instruction and resources, the smarter one becomes within that area of intelligence.

Each Intelligence Involves Subabilities or Different Manifestations

No one is simply "musically" or "linguistically" intelligent. One's musical intelligence might be demonstrated through the ability to compose clever tunes or to hear and distinguish instrument parts in a song. In the case of linguistic intelligence, ability might emerge through creative writing, word play (poetry), closing arguments in the courtroom, or acting in a play. Strengths are demonstrated through end states or domains.

Intelligences Work in Combination in Domains, Not Isolation

As described earlier, each intelligence is relatively autonomous in its "raw" state. Each intelligence represents a different way of thinking, solving problems, and learning. Although each intelligence operates relatively independently—that is, the brain has distinct mechanisms and operations for each intelligence—in reality they work in combination, in the context of a domain or discipline. The distinction between intelligences and domains becomes clear when one considers that effective work in any domain is realized through the use of several intelligences.

Intelligence refers to biological and psychological potential and abilities, whereas domains or disciplines are social constructs. Whereas intelligence is the raw material we bring to bear in solving problems or fashioning products, domains are culturally organized and valued activities "in which individuals participate on more than just a casual basis, and in which degrees of expertise can be identified and nurtured" (Gardner, 1999, p. 82). Computer programming, car mechanics, gardening, and soccer are all examples of domains.

For example, a violinist needs musical intelligence to be successful, but only in combination with interpersonal abilities, such as communication with other musicians in the orchestra; intrapersonal, such as translating the emotion of the piece; and bodily-kinesthetic, such as the physical act of playing the instrument. Put simply, the musical domain generally requires high levels of musical intelligence, but other intelligences must be tapped to perform successfully in this domain.

Similarly, a particular intelligence like spatial intelligence is not isolated to a specific domain, such as the arts. Indeed, any particular intelligence can be applied in many domains. In the case of spatial intelligence, these abilities come to the fore in the arts, as well as sailing, gardening, and even surgery. An individual's strength in a particular intelligence may manifest itself in one (or more) domain and not others. For example, someone with a high level of spatial aptitude may have little ability or interest in the artistic domain and may be attracted to more scientific applications of spatial intelligence embedded in, say, biology or topology.

The Journey From Theory to Practice

[Multiple intelligences] is not a technique, it's a mind set.
~ Helen Sablan, AMI Pilot Teacher

Introduction

As a theory, MI does not prescribe any particular approach or activities. Rather, classroom practices are based on an understanding of what such a theory of intelligence suggests and how it can inform practice. Just as practices in today's schools are rooted in the conventional wisdom of intelligence, an understanding of intelligence from the perspective of MI theory has its own set of implications for the classroom. In other words, the educator asks herself, "If intelligence is as MI theory describes it, then what does that imply for how I set up my classroom, how I approach instruction, and what activities I make available to my students?"

There is indeed no single right way to apply MI theory, but using MI theory as a "lens" or "mind set" in the classroom can and has helped inform excellent, and often quite distinct, teaching and learning practices. Because it is an act of interpretation from a theory of intelligence to actual classroom practices, applying MI theory in the classroom provokes a critical process of practice and reflection on the part of the educator. Teachers decide for themselves how to apply it, reflecting and making revisions and additions along the way.

Many educators have enthusiastically accepted the challenge of creating and implementing applications for MI theory. For many of them, MI theory confirms what they have always believed: Students possess a range of abilities that standard classroom fare neither acknowledges, celebrates, nor nurtures.

> This theory provides the means to articulate beliefs about my teaching that I've always held dear, but had a limited vocabulary to express.... It provides a well-defined vision of the breadth of [students'] strengths and where we might find them. (Robert Bickerton, Director of Adult Education, Massachusetts Department of Education, personal communication, June 1, 2000)

MI Goes to School

Several models and approaches have been developed to apply MI theory into practice in K–8 classrooms (Baum, Viens, & Slatin, in press; Faculty of the New City School, 1994; Kornhaber & Fierros, 2000). Since the start of the AMI Study, we found that no existing model offered a proper fit with the goals and contexts of adult basic education. Accordingly, we (the AMI research team) articulated a model of MI application in adult basic education contexts based on the classroom efforts of the AMI teachers to apply MI theory and guided by the Pathways model developed by Baum and her colleagues.

We identified four distinct approaches for MI application in adult basic education (Figure 1.3): MI Reflections, Bridging Students' Areas of Strengths to Areas of Challenge, Entry/Exit Points, and Projects. Although we use different terminology, our designation for each approach was influenced by the Pathways model for applying MI theory in the elementary classroom: Explorations, Building on Strengths, Understanding, and Authentic Problems. (A fifth pathway, Talent Development, does not have an analogous cohort in adult basic education.) Like the Pathways, each of the AMI approaches is tied to specific goals for using MI theory. Our somewhat different terminology reflects the fact that the goals for using MI theory in adult basic education are similar to those sought in elementary education but not exactly like them.

We discuss the AMI model and its four different approaches to applying MI theory in this chapter. Each approach is described below in terms of its primary goal, the theoretical features of MI in which the practice is rooted, and examples from AMI teachers to their classrooms. Where relevant, myths or misconceptions about MI theory related to that approach are described

MI Reflections

The intelligences describe the "smarts" that students bring to the learning context, each student possessing a unique amalgam of intelligences that distinguishes him or her from the others. The focus of an MI Reflections approach to applying MI is getting to know students through an MI lens, that is, identifying their strengths and interests.

MI theory provides the vocabulary for articulating observations and descriptions of students' strengths and interests. An MI-based description of students' preferred intelligences presents a stark contrast to a numerical IQ measurement, particularly in terms of its usefulness ("What do I do with the information?"). With MI theory, the question moves from "How smart are you?" (a 70 IQ, a 120 IQ) to "How are you smart?" (I can take anything apart, fix it, and put it back together. I have an amazing backhand. I make hats.).

In the AMI Study, MI Reflections (MIR) referred to strategies or activities that used MI theory to better know and understand students (see Chapter 2). MIR was applied in two different ways, each with a different emphasis. In one approach the teacher observed her students and identified their strengths and preferences by noting patterns over time in the course of observations. The second approach put students at the center of the reflection process, with the goal being for the students to "own" their intelligences and see themselves as intelligent people with a variety of abilities.

MI theory says that intelligence is demonstrated in real world contexts, in the problems individuals solve and the things they make. Therefore, an MI-based perspective on assessment—including the observation and identification of student strengths—would suggest assessment that involves observing individual students, amidst authentic uses of their "smarts." AMI teacher Terri Coustan observed her students, jotting down notes that she later organized by student, so that she could identify patterns of behavior and preferences for each of them. She observed them across a range of activities, including gardening projects, computing, art activities, building projects, and basic literacy activities.

Figure 1.3. How Teachers Apply MI Theory

MI Reflections

- Uses MI theory as a basis to reflect on and identify students' strengths and preferences.
- Emphasizes student participation in MI-based self-reflections.

Bridging Students' Areas of Strengths to Areas of Challenge

- Creates a "bridge" from students' MI strengths to appropriate learning strategies.
- Emphasizes using students' particular strengths to assist in areas of particular difficulty.

Entry/Exit Points

- Provide a range of MI-informed ways to introduce and explore a topic (entry points) and for students to demonstrate their learning of the topic (exit points).
- Develop or use entry and exit points that tap into students' strengths.

Projects

- Develop project-based curriculum using MI theory as a framework.
- Emphasize authentic problems and activities.

MI theory also claims that intelligence is learnable; we can get smarter. In other words, our profiles of intelligence change. Moreover, a single intelligence can manifest itself across a number of domains. Thus, knowing students means watching them grow, get better, and develop new or renewed interests. MI observations might best be described as peering through MI lenses in an ongoing quest to "catch students at their best." Observations are informal, over time, and across different contexts.

Another approach to MIR puts students at the center of the reflection process, providing the tools and opportunities for self-reflection and understanding their own unique collections of strengths and preferences. Basic adult education students often see themselves as failures, having low self-esteem and feelings of incompetence when it comes to school. Teachers use MI to counter this negative self-perception, to bolster students' self-esteem through reflection activities that identify and validate students' strengths. Teachers provide different ways for students to understand and articulate their own strengths, such as paper/pencil surveys, journal reflections, or postactivity discussions, and other hands-on activities that call on students to use and reflect on their strengths (see Chapter 2). With these activities, students face substantive evidence that they are smart and have the tools and knowledge to articulate how.

Several AMI teachers used MI self-reflection surveys and other activities to help students see and believe their intelligences (see Chapter 2). Meg Costanzo used dialogue journals that included student reflections about their strengths. Wendy Quiñones had students debrief about a film they watched together, each drawing on observations based on personal strengths.

Knowing their students from the perspective of their strengths and interests becomes a primary source from which teachers identify learning strategies and activities that map onto students' strength areas and interests. Any information culled from student reflection activities—that is, students' own understandings of their strengths and preferences—can and should be used to inform the curriculum and instruction. Thus MIR is also the first step to personalizing instruction and curriculum for students.

MI Reflections: Myths and Misconceptions

Unfortunately, some individuals have translated MIR or assessment into eight (or nine) tests, one for each intelligence, setting MI theory within a conventional understanding of assessing intelligence through paper-and-pencil tests. This is problematic on at least two fronts.

First, it assumes that intelligence can be properly or fully assessed using the paper-and-pencil, multiple-choice mode, which reflects a psychometric view of intelligence that is contrary to MI theory. Within the framework of MI theory, no single paper-and-pencil test can assess the breadth and depth of any individual's intelligence.

Second, this misconception assumes that one can come up with a definitive assessment of an individual's intelligences. It is probably not possible, and certainly not practical, to pursue definitive or final assessments of students' intelligences. Each intelligence includes subabilities, each suggesting different ways a student might demonstrate one form of intelligence. Moreover, there are too many different domains in which particular students might demonstrate one or another intelligence. For example, only by looking at art activities, you miss the spatial abilities of the builder or the photographer. In other words, there is too much ground to cover for a truly definitive assessment of any individual's unique collection of intelligences.

Getting an accurate "reading" of the ways an individual is intelligent would require using an extensive array of assessment activities to ensure a comprehensive assessment. An individual would likely have strengths that any single or small collection of assessments (or observation events) would not gauge. Again, this is a classic case of new wine in an old bottle; an understanding of intelligence as static and measurable is transferred to MI theory.

Another less pervasive, but more disconcerting, myth is that MI theory validates cultural and racial stereotypes. MI theory is quite to the contrary and serves to disaggregate individuals within the same cultural or racial groupings, rather than aggregating cultural or racial groups by intelligences (and intelligence levels). MI theory should not be used to label one group as naturally better or worse at one intelligence or the other. As human beings, we are all at promise for all intelligences. The form intelligences take might be culturally defined, but the extent to which any individual of a given racially or culturally defined group possesses a particular intelligence is not culturally defined. Put simply, race and culture do not determine in what ways and how smart an individual is (Gray & Viens, 1994).

Bridging Students' Areas of Strengths to Areas of Challenge

In some cases, teachers use MI to develop activities and learning strategies that are tailored to students' strengths. In this case the teacher's goal is to apply her understanding of MI theory—and of her students' particular strengths and preferences—to develop different ways to engage students in a particular topic or skill. Teachers are always seeking ways to involve and to reach and teach more of their students. Developing ways to approach a topic or skill area that draws on students' particular strengths and interests can help them do so. (Approaches based on this bridging idea can be found in Chapter 3.)

Using the information culled in MI Reflections, teachers identify related learning strategies for individuals or groups of students. For example, through her ongoing observations and analysis, or pattern finding, Terri Coustan, came up with language arts strategies that connected with her students' musical and spatial abilities. In one case, Terri developed chants to help a student—who used chants as a shaman—to learn vocabulary words. In the second case, several students were able to find or create spatial representations of words they were learning. Some students found photographs in magazines that depicted particular vocabulary words; others made scenes or figures out of clay to represent new words. The students' work— photograph collages and sculptures—also helped Terri determine whether her students had an accurate understanding of the words.

Working with students one or two at a time, Betsy Cornwell was able to observe which strategies were working with her students, which ones were not, and change the latter accordingly. In one lesson, Betsy was able to offer a more hands-on, bodily-kinesthetic and spatial approach to subtraction for one student, using beans and plates, while the other found it easier to use the traditional paper-and-pencil method. Meg Costanzo used students' own reflections and self-described strengths to work with them in constructing appropriate ways for each student to learn the material at hand. For example, Meg helped one student, a carpenter, rally his spatial skills to set up and solve math problems visually/spatially.

Bridging Students' Areas of Strengths to Areas of Challenge: Myths and Misconceptions

MI theory is often confused with learning styles. MI theory suggests that people respond, individually, in different ways, to different kinds of content, such as music or language or other people. MI theory describes the different ways in which people process information as well as the types of problems they process and products they create. This is very different from the notion of a learning style. Learning styles refer to different ways of receiving information, in terms of sensory modalities (e.g., auditory, visual, or tactile) and social contexts (i.e., extrovert, introvert, field-sensitive, or field-independent). Learning styles refer to global preferences in how we take in information. In other words, individuals are described as being "auditory" learners or "visual" learners regardless of the task at hand.

Consider a poem. How a person "takes in" the poem is a stylistic dimension. That is, whether one reads the poem, hears it, sits in a favorite chair, or reads the poem first thing in the morning because one is a "morning person," all of these refer back to learning styles and to preference. However, how one processes and makes meaning of the poem taps into the individual's multiple intelligences. For example, one might focus on powerful words in the poem, imagine the subject or an image representative of the work. One might focus on the shape of the poem—where the line breaks occur. These are examples of how MI theory, the intelligences, works to process the poem and to develop one's understanding of it.

Gardner (1999) points out that there is little evidence to suggest that a person who uses or prefers one style in one context will use the same style in another or all other contexts. The link between MI theory and learning styles needs to be worked out empirically, on a style-by-style basis. Consider the example of an individual who has difficulty learning from the spoken word. Meetings, conferences, and classrooms where lecture is primary all present a challenge to this person's learning. However, if music or sound effects are the auditory content, this individual is a quick study. In this case, it would be inaccurate to label this person globally as an "auditory" learner.

In summary, MI theory is distinct from learning styles in at least two major ways:

o   MI theory refers to the ways we process and make meaning of different kinds of content, whereas learning styles refer to modes of receiving information.

o   Learning styles are used as global descriptors, whereas MI theory varies with the domain or content in question.

Entry Points and Exit Points

MI theory's most distinguishing characteristic, that intelligence is pluralistic, suggests creating for students a context for a broad range of experiences—in domains and across intelligences. MI theory also serves as a framework to organize and develop those diverse learning experiences, commonly referred to as "entry points" or "exit points." Entry points refer to how students engage in the subject or content, in other words, the activities in which they participate. Exit points refer to what they do to demonstrate their learning, in other words, how students' learning is assessed. Building MI-based entry and exit points is a common starting point for many teachers new to MI theory.

MI theory becomes a lens onto teachers' classroom offerings through which teachers identify strengths and gaps. Giving students a number of choices based on MI theory is widely used by teachers as a vehicle to provide different entry and exit points for students. For example, Martha Jean gave her students different learning options related to specific GED-related content.

Entry Points and Exit Points: Myths and Misconceptions

A popular myth has developed, which goes something like this: "If there are eight different intelligences, then I need to teach everything at least eight different ways." Every lesson becomes a round-robin of MI activities. The more fitting question is, "How can I use MI theory to help my students learn about '…' or learn how to '…'?"

Intelligences should not be the goal of the lesson but the means to the learning goals. Trying to do everything eight different ways puts getting all the intelligences "in" at the top of the priority list, to the detriment of learning goals. Furthermore, intelligences work in combination, within a domain. A lesson in the science domain requires, but is not limited to, logical-mathematical intelligence. Dividing all lessons into eight intelligence-based experiences is inauthentic to how intelligences really work.

Projects

Multiple intelligences describes the "tools" people bring to any task. Intelligence is couched in what people can do and make, in the problems they solve. Therefore, in many MI classrooms, MI theory has been translated into the implementation of authentic curricula, such as problem-based curriculum and projects that, at the very least, simulate real world activities. The assumption is that students will engage and learn more successfully if provided with opportunities to solve real problems and make real things. Teachers have found that providing authentic learning opportunities also gives them a chance to see students in new contexts and perhaps to observe student strengths that have as of yet remained untapped.

Meg Costanzo had students participate in a real recruitment project at the Tutorial Center, each taking on one or more tasks to increase student enrollment at the center (which they did). For example, one student developed a public service announcement that was used on a local radio station. Other students worked on changing the sign in front of the Tutorial Center. They dealt with everything from zoning to phrasing in order to post a new sign that would attract new students. Terri Coustan used projects that built on her students' real projects at home. For example, she was able to secure a plot in a community garden for her students, almost all of whom were avid gardeners. This project included not only the naturalist intelligence but required the interpersonal, spatial, and bodily-kinesthetic abilities needed to share and tend to the garden.

Conclusion

What these approaches to MI application have in common is that they are rooted in an understanding of MI theory, its major features, its implications for teaching and learning, and a desire to know and use students' intelligences. It is important to note that these approaches are not mutually exclusive. In fact, all the AMI teachers tried different interpretations of MI theory consecutively or in tandem.

Terri Coustan observed students over time (MI Reflections), instituted student options that gave students different entry points into the lessons (Entry Points), and offered student-centered projects, such as gardening (Projects). Over time and through their explorations, AMI teachers settled on MI applications that responded to their needs and goals, worked well in practice, and received positive responses from students.

MI theory did not direct the AMI teachers to any particular teaching techniques, but it served as a catalyst in their MI journeys. MI theory offers a framework and a language to develop practices that best fit one's context while acknowledging, celebrating, and building on the abilities adult students bring to their learning.

Chapter 1 Reflection and Discussion Questions

o   What is your opinion of MI theory's definition of intelligence?

o   How is the traditional view of intelligence reflected in your teaching or the requirements your students must meet?

o   What evidence have you seen in your learners that supports the idea that there are many ways to be "smart"?

o   What implications do you think MI theory has for teaching and learning?

Working From Strengths/Working From Weaknesses: MI Experiences in the Classroom

Susan Baum, a researcher and teacher–educator, developed this simulation and provided staff development on MI-based instruction for the AMI teachers. She designed this activity to help contrast the learning experiences of students' working and communicating in ways that align with their profiles of intelligences, versus students' experiences when they are working in areas of relative weakness.

Ideally, about 25 participants are needed for this activity. Tables and additional space for one of the groups to work are also needed. Participants should not read the directions before engaging in the activity.

Directions for the Activity Facilitator

Discuss how each individual has preferred modes of solving a problem and developing products. Some are at their best when they can visualize a solution to a problem and communicate through the visual arts. Others may prefer the performing arts, writing, or building and design. In this activity, participants rate their self-efficacy or perceived ability or level of development in each of the following domains: writing, drawing, performing arts, and building. Each person rank orders the following four choices in terms of level of talent or expertise, with 1 being the most expert and 4 being the most novice. A facilitator needs to record the number of responses for each group because he or she will need this information to form groups later. After you have completed your rankings, complete Figure 2.3.

There are two parts, or experiences, to this simulation. Experience 1 involves grouping participants into novice groups (domain area that is least preferred). Experience 2 involves grouping participants into expert groups (domain area most preferred). The ideal number of participants in each group should range from 4 to 10. If a group is too large, consider splitting the group in half or having some people switch to their second/most preferred or second/least preferred choice.

Once you have a sense of the choices of the participants, you are ready to begin the simulation. Imagine you are in your ABE class and will be working on group projects. The class has been studying Healthy Living, and each group is required to create a product that demonstrates three aspects of healthy living. (Note that the project topic can be changed and related specifically to ongoing topics in your classroom.) Group participants according to your novice or least preferred talent (# 4 preference) and use that form of expression for your product. In summary, there should be four groups who receive the directions as shown in Figure 2.4.

Figure 2.3. Tally Sheet

	Tally
Who listed drawing first?	_____
Who listed building first?	_____
Who listed writing first?	_____
Who listed performing first?	_____
Who listed drawing last?	_____
Who listed building last?	_____
Who listed writing last?	_____
Who listed performing last?	_____

Figure 2.4. Preference Groupings

Group	Materials	Products
Writing	Paper and Pencil	Must be written down
Drawing	Transparencies or paper, markers	Must be illustrated without verbal, written, or oral explanations
Building	LEGO ® bricks and accessories	Must build without verbal explanations
Performing	Space (outside the classroom)	Must be a performance (talk is permitted, but "answers" cannot be stated)

The group "passes" if the rest of the class can recognize the three aspects of healthy living; they "fail" if their classmates cannot recognize them.

Assign an observer to each group. Observers can be recruited from the larger groups. Allow each group about 10 to 15 minutes to complete its product. The observer records (a) time on task, (b) group dynamics, (c) avoidance behaviors, (d) level of enthusiasm, (e) the group's standards for success, and any other observations about the group's process.

When the time is up, each group shares its product. The performing arts group performs in front of the audience, the drawing group shares its drawings, the writers read their written product, and the builders display their product. After each presentation, the audience is asked to identify the aspects of healthy living each group has presented. After all the products are shared, the observers from each group share their observations.

The process is repeated. This time the participants are regrouped into their preferred or "expert" area. The instructions remain the same. The observers remain with their initial assigned area so that they are able to compare the differences in the process when participants are working in an area of strength as compared to a novice or least preferred area. More time may be needed as the groups will tend to be more elaborate and have higher standards for success.

Upon completion of the products, have the groups share their work and the observers present their findings as in the first group activity.

Discussion Questions

You may want to continue the discussion with the following questions.

1. In which situation did you rely more on your group as a necessary support?

2. Which experience resulted in a product that showed the most attention to detail?

3. How might the quality of the product affect your assessment of the participants' knowledge of the topic?

4. Which situation caused more stress for you?

Debriefing for Facilitator

You are likely to find that the second set of products is superior to the first. It appears that the second group knew more about healthy living than the first group. In reality, the knowledge level did not change. What did change was the avenue through which the participants were allowed to express their knowledge of healthy living. In the first activity, the groups were limited by their ability to draw, write, build, or perform. For instance, they may have known that regular exercise is key to good health but did not know how to draw a picture of a figure in action. The second group, however, was able to draw what they needed to in order to make their point.

It is crucial to conduct a discussion in which you compare your experiences in both activities. You may want to cover the following aspects of the experience: role of the group, creativity, enthusiasm, time on task, noise level, quality of the product, level of details, and level of knowledge.

In most cases, the role of the group in the first experience is supportive. People in this group understand the benefits of working with other novices to the domain. In the second experience, the members of the group are more independent and confident, and may prefer to work on their own. Creativity is used differently in both experiences. In the first, it is used to avoid the task or to find clever ways to compensate for lack of talent. In the second experience, the creativity is shown in the enhancement and quality of the product. Participant enthusiasm is usually much higher in the second experience. However, on occasion, in the second activity the participants feel pressured to be perfect because they have admitted that they are talented in this area. In the first experience, they perceived the expectation to be much lower, whereas in actuality, the criteria for passing the task remained the same. As will become evident, the time on task will greatly increase when students are working in their talent area. Likewise, the quality of the products in the second part of the simulation will be superior to those in the first part. Most interesting, the knowledge the participants display about healthy living will seem greater during the second part. The participants will tend to go beyond the minimal expectations of the assignment.

Sharing Something I Do Well

Meg Costanzo developed this lesson to help her students learn how to organize information for essay writing, as well as to stimulate a discussion about their strongest intelligences.

Subject Writing
Time 45 minutes to 1 hour
Materials Paper, pens, pencils, example of something you personally do well (e.g., food specialties you make, woodworking or needlework projects you have created, a musical performance you could share, and so on)

Background

I have used this writing assignment twice with adult learners attending GED/ Diploma classes; both times it led to intense writing sessions where students wrote extensive essays about things they do well. Besides providing students with the opportunity to practice their writing skills, this assignment also gave me valuable information regarding my students' strongest intelligences.

The Lesson

Getting Started

At the beginning of the lesson, I asked the students to list the things that they do well, including things they enjoy doing or things for which they have received compliments from others. I gave them examples from a wide range of activities: cooking, being a good friend, sports, hobbies, work-related activities, and so on. I encouraged them to think of anything at all that came to mind.

Modeling Technique

After the students finished writing their lists, I shared with them something that I do well. I brought in some of the cross-stitch work that I have done, showing the class samples of framed pictures, projects presently in the works, kits, materials, instructions, and so on.

I then asked the students to generate a list of questions that they had for me regarding what I had just shared with them. We listed the questions on the board. When the students were finished with this activity, I went back and answered their questions, writing my replies next to each one. Working from student feedback, we organized this information into a logical order as it might appear in an essay about something I do well.

Brainstorming

At this point, I had each student select one response from the lists that had been generated at the beginning of the session. Working in small groups or with partners, the students wrote lists of questions for each other around these topics. After the students generated questions for their classmates, I gave them the opportunity to add more questions to their own personal lists. In a sense, the students interviewed themselves at this stage of the writing exercise.

Writing

Then the students answered their own list of questions. After finishing this part of the assignment, the students went on to organize the information they had written into a logical sequence and, finally, to write an essay about something they do well.

Reflections and Student Responses

This prewriting exercise enabled the students to generate a lot of information to include in their essays. It encouraged the students to use a self-interview technique when brainstorming. This has proven particularly helpful with reluctant writers who do not know where to begin when faced with a writing assignment.

When I was sharing this lesson with a group of my colleagues, one instructor stopped me at the beginning of my presentation and asked how this lesson was dissimilar from a typical prewriting exercise. I think that it is important for educators to realize that MI-inspired lessons may not be radically different from the types of lessons that they had previously taught; instead, the lessons may simply contain new elements that have been informed by MI theory. A number of things were different about this lesson compared with how I might have presented it previously:

1. I brought in my needlework project to show the class, instead of just telling them about my hobby.

2. I modeled the prewriting technique for the students.

3. Students used interviews to gather information during the prewriting phase of the

exercise, as opposed to merely listing information on a "web" independently.

4. I encouraged the students to bring in samples of things they do well and share them with the other students.

From an MI standpoint, the assignment provided me with a wealth of information about the students. I learned many new things about my students that I may never have known without having done this assignment with them. It should be noted, however, that it is not advisable to have the students work on this essay until you have had time to establish a comfortable sense of community within the classroom.

Memory Lane

Jean Mantzaris wanted to find a way to incorporate MI theory into her work as a career counselor with adult students. The results of her efforts are the following two lessons. They are designed to encourage students to reflect upon their strongest intelligences and then use this self-understanding to identify those jobs for which they might be best suited.

Subject   Career Counseling
Time   1 to 2 hours
Materials Variety of props (LEGO® bricks, blocks, puppets, art supplies, other toys)
Students provide stories, songs, photos, and props reminiscent of their favorite childhood activities.
Manila shipping tags with reinforced hole (2 3/4 by 1 3/8 inches)
Markers, pens, pictures, glue, and other art materials for the students to use when they decorate their key-chain ornaments

Background

I designed this lesson for ABE/GED students to help them focus their thoughts as they begin the career decision-making process. Prior to this activity, the students had assessed themselves using my colleague's AMI Survey: "How Are You Smart?" (presented later in this chapter). They became familiar with readings and visuals that described Gardner's theory and the eight intelligences. Using information from the survey, each student created his or her individual multiple intelligences profile. The students and I also compiled this information about the students' strongest and weakest intelligences into a class profile.

I divided our classroom space into a discussion area and a separate "play" area. The play area contained props and materials we had brought into class.

The Lesson

My goal for this lesson was to encourage the students to reflect upon their childhood intelligences and determine if there were any links between childhood and adult intelligences.

Introduction

I reminded the students that they had already learned about their strengths or intelligences and we had discussed how this self-knowledge might aid them in the career decision-making process. After thanking the students for all the materials they had brought in to share with the class, I asked them to pretend to go back in time and think about activities that they loved to do as children. Encouraging each student to participate, I led a discussion about this topic. The students then responded to this question: "How do the activities we loved as kids connect to our adult strengths?"

As a group, we shared possible reasons why a person's childhood intelligences might not have flourished as he or she grew older. Some of the answers the class came up with included economic disadvantages, different values on the part of their parents, and physical or psychological abuse. I shared with the students the story of Maya Angelou who did not speak for many years because she had been threatened by a person who had abused her. I suggested that the students read her book, *I Know Why the Caged Bird Sings*. I also gave examples of other famous people, like Grandma Moses, who made great accomplishments later in life.

Students Share Favorite Childhood Activities

At that point, we went over to our play area. I asked the students to spend about 20 minutes playing. As they played, I asked them to think about how and if their childhood intelligences were connected to their adult intelligences. I encouraged the students to focus on those activities in which they were most interested. As I observed the students and wandered about the "playscape," I indulged myself and played with some activities that appealed to me.

Connecting Then to Now

We went back to the discussion area of the room, where I posed these questions for discussion:

- o Which favorite activities were connected to something you currently do?

- o Are there some activities from your childhood that you are interested in continuing or becoming better at?

- o Do they pose any implications for a possible career?

Finally, I asked the students each to select a strength or intelligence that they would like to nurture.

Construction of "Awakening" Key Chain Ornament

I told the class that I had chosen to have them make key chains because most adults have keys to apartments, cars, and so on, and a key is used for opening or starting something. In a sense, the students were opening their minds to new ideas or starting to think about a career.

I handed out the manila shipping tags. I asked the students to design an "Awakening" key chain ornament representing an intelligence that they would choose to reawaken or reaffirm. The students thought about possible designs and made their ornaments at home or in the next class. I then laminated the finished ornaments.

Journal Writing

Before the close of class, I asked the students to comment in their journals about their childhood intelligences and possible connections to adult strengths and career choices. Most important, I asked them to respond to this question, "What did you learn today?"

Reflections and Student Responses

It was interesting to see the types of things the students brought into class as representations of their favorite childhood activities. One student brought in some fishing equipment; another brought in the materials and loom used to weave potholders. Gathering all the materials became a collaborative effort. One student mentioned that he would like to have some masks in the play area, so I brought in some from home. Other members of my program's faculty and staff also became involved. The secretary brought in musical instruments; another teacher collected some action figures for the class to use. Someone else brought in the game Parcheesi®.

My students were very willing to participate in the play activities, connect the way they were to the way they are, and relate these strengths to possible careers. This activity raised the level of career decision-making to a new high; it really put the "me" into the process. It provided a significant addition to our program that already included such other career decision-making activities as taking an interest inventory, exploring careers, and looking at values and achievement.

The student who had asked me to bring in some masks had also brought in a picture of himself as a youngster dressed in a Halloween costume. His comments regarding this activity underscore the value it can have in promoting career decision-making: "When I was younger, my imagination could make anything out of nothing. I see myself doing some of that now, and I'd like to take a look at this."

MI Bingo

Susan Baum and Julie Viens use a game based on the popular bingo format to set the stage for discussion about MI theory. This activity works especially well as an icebreaker with a new group of students who are just meeting for the first time.

> I felt like I really got to know people today and that helps me overcome my shyness.
>
> ~ Student of AMI Pilot Teacher Helen Sablan about doing MI Bingo

Distribute a bingo card to each student (Figure 2.5). Tell students that they are to circulate around the room and get others to sign their cards. Signers may write their name in any box that applies to them but can only sign a single slot once. This part of the activity is complete when the first person who collects five signed boxes across, down, or diagonally calls out "Bingo." (You might want to have an inexpensive prize available for the winner.)

Discuss the relationship of individuals' strengths (where they signed) and the intelligences they used for those activities.

MI Personal Graph

Reviewing the statements in the left-hand column of the personal MI Graph (Figure 2.6), the students circle any items under the Activity/Ability heading that apply to themselves. They may add two others at the bottom, if they feel their favorite activities or areas of strength are not already represented on the list. The students then think about why and how they are good at that activity/ability, checking off those intelligences that they think come into play. The students can check off as many intelligences as they wish. For instance, someone who selected garden/farm might check off these intelligences for the following reasons:

Naturalist: "I enjoy selecting which plants will work best in a particular location."

Bodily-Kinesthetic: "I like to get my hands in the dirt."

Intrapersonal: "It's the time when I get to reflect upon things."

After completing the grid, the students can tally up the number of responses they have for each intelligence or simply look for patterns that might indicate their intelligence strengths. Students can share their reflections in dialogue journals, learning logs, or through group discussions. Additionally, you might ask students to bring in some objects or representations of their favorite activities to share with the class. MI Bingo and MI Personal Graph work well to introduce MI to colleagues.

Figure 2.5. MI Bingo Card

Draw or paint	Study maps	Play musical instrument	Keep a diary	Crossword puzzle fan
Speak in public	Dance	Take photos	Give advice and support	Read biographies
Do logical puzzles	Garden/farm	Read/write poetry	Act in theatrical productions	Sing
Do volunteer work in the community	Sculpt or carve	Build/renovate	Write songs	Spend time outdoors
Take care of kids	Athlete/play sports	Do crafts	Can say "no"	Family "accountant"

Figure 2.6. Personal MI Graph

Activity/ability	Naturalist	Linguistic	Logical-Math	Interpersonal	Intrapersonal	Spatial	Bodily-Kinesthetic	Musical
Family "accountant"								
Do logical puzzles								
Sing								
Speak in public								
Read biographies								
Crossword puzzle fan								
Keep a diary								
Give advice and support								
Spend time outdoors								
Act in theatrical productions								
Write songs								
Do crafts								
Build/renovate								
Read/write poetry								
Take photos								
Take care of kids								
Study maps								
Do volunteer work in the community								
Can say "no"								
Athlete/ play sports								
Dance								
Draw or paint								
Garden/farm								
Play musical instrument								
Sculpt or carve								

AMI Survey: "How Are You Smart?"

Meg Costanzo developed this AMI assessment survey as a way for students to learn about MI theory while exploring their own particular MI profiles. In developing it, she was influenced by *Seven Kinds of Smart* by Thomas Armstrong (1993) and *Stepping Stones: A MIDAS Workbook for the Multiple Intelligences* by Branton Shearer (1994).

Working on their own, students listen to a taped version of the AMI Survey: "How Are You Smart?" that contains statements specific to each of the eight intelligences. As the students listen to the tape, they can follow along on a written version of the survey, if they so desire. After hearing each scenario, the students respond by circling the appropriate phrase on the response form (Figure 2.7), determining whether the statements describe them "very much," "a lot," "somewhat," "a little," or "hardly at all."

Prepare students to take this survey by going over the response form with them beforehand. Have the students do a practice response by showing them a number of statements such as, "My favorite season is winter. I like pizza. I'd rather read than watch TV. I like to go camping. I hate housecleaning. I am a morning person."

Ask each student how he or she might respond to these statements as a whole by choosing one of the five phrases listed above. Suggest that the students choose "somewhat" if about half the statements pertain to them. Encourage the students to go with their gut reaction rather than to labor over their responses.

After completing the survey, the students graph their responses on a grid (Figure 2.8). This grid contains only the x and y axes because this exercise is also intended to be a math lesson; students are encouraged to develop their own ways to graphically represent their responses.

Use this exercise as a springboard to discuss MI theory and the implications it might have for adult students as learners. Remember that this is not a scientific assessment tool but rather an entertaining exercise to help students begin reflecting upon their intelligence strengths.

Some teachers who have tried using this survey with their classes have found it more advisable to present students with a more structured form of the graph, one that shows discrete boxes for each possible response. The students then simply check off the eight boxes that correspond to their responses.

AMI pilot teacher Helen Sablan found it easier for her students to take the AMI Assessment Survey when it was presented in the form of a checklist. She listed each statement separately. The students checked off those statements that they felt applied to them. Because this is not a scientific assessment tool with an equal number of equally weighted statements in each category, teachers are advised not to try to quantify the student results too exactly. This method of data collection, however, can be quite helpful in generating interest in MI theory and encouraging students to begin reflecting upon their intelligence strengths.

The following pages can be copied for use with students and others.

How Are You Smart?

Introduction

Most people are smarter than they think. This is because people typically think of intelligence just as having a high IQ or getting good grades in school. However, there are many ways that people can be intelligent.

In order to help you learn what is needed to pass the GED tests or to earn an Adult Diploma, I need to know something about you. This survey will help us learn the different ways that you are intelligent. From this information, we will be able to plan lessons that will help you learn as quickly and easily as possible by using your "smarts."

Please take the time to listen to each of the eight selections on the tape. At the pause after each selection, circle the response that you feel best describes you. If about half of the statements apply to you, circle "somewhat" as your response. Every item in a selection does not have to be true about you to mark "very much." If you want to hear the selection again, feel free to rewind the tape. You can also follow along a written script of the tape, if you so desire.

Remember that there are no right or wrong answers to this survey. Each individual is different. I want to find out what your interests and abilities are, and use that information to guide our lessons.

Selection #1

I enjoy singing and listening to music. I can tell when a person is singing or playing a musical instrument off key. I find it easy to sing along to a song after hearing it just a couple of times. When I am home or in the car, I usually have music playing. I sound great when I'm singing in the shower. I know how to play a musical instrument, or I'd like to learn how to play one. I have a large collection of CDs or tapes. When I'm driving in a car or working, I find myself humming, singing, or tapping my fingers to the beat. I enjoyed taking music classes in school. I was in my school band or chorus. I feel I could have been a musician if I had put my mind to it. I think I would enjoy a career that involves music. I can't imagine my life without music.

Selection #2

I enjoy at least one of these activities: sports, dance, handicrafts, walking, running, or exercise. I think of myself as being well coordinated. I like working with my hands. I enjoy activities like needlework or woodworking, where I can make something, and I do a good job. I belonged to sports teams when I was in school. I was in plays when I was in school. Time permitting, I would consider joining a local theater group. I can pick up new dance steps easily. I'm a "hands-on" learner. I learn best by practicing a new skill rather than by reading a manual or watching a video. I'd rather do physical work than sit at a desk for long periods of time. I like being on the go. I find physical activity inspiring. I often come up with creative ideas while doing something physical. I would prefer a career that allowed me to be active.

Selection #3

I enjoy reading. I am comfortable speaking in front of others. I frequently write notes and checklists for myself. I enjoy poetry, storytelling, or reading aloud. I have at least one favorite author. I have a library card. I subscribe to a newspaper or magazine. I prefer learning something new by reading written directions. I like to write letters to family members and friends. When I hear a new word, I'm curious to find out what it means. I enjoy playing word games like Scrabble® or Password™. In school, I did better in English and social studies than I did in math and science. When I am reading an article or book that has many pictures, I tend to concentrate more on the words than on the illustrations. When I want to learn something new, I will read up on the subject first. I'd like to have a career that involves writing.

Selection #4

I enjoy working with numbers. I enjoyed taking math and science classes in school. I'm good at problem-solving and reasoning. I like to set up step-by-step methods to finish a project or meet a goal. I like to organize things in a logical way. I enjoy balancing my checkbook. I find it easy to remember telephone numbers. I can really make a good case to back up my opinions when I am arguing with someone. I play chess or other games that require logical strategy. I read mysteries and try to figure out the ending myself. I love to work on crossword puzzles. I have a computer that I use frequently, or I am interested in getting a computer. I'd like to find a job that involves working with numbers or in science.

Selection #5

I enjoy drawing, photography, model making, or other arts or crafts. I am good at reading maps and have a better than average sense of direction. I pay attention to colors and am good at matching things. I'm a detail-oriented person. When I am asked to explain something, I will draw a sketch. I think in pictures. When I'm talking on the telephone or listening to others, I catch myself doodling. I can fix and assemble things easily. I can look at something and see how it works. Rather than follow written directions, I'd rather learn by looking at an example of what has to be done. I often remember dreams vividly. I prefer reading material that has many illustrations that go along with the text. I enjoyed taking art classes in school. I think I'd like a career where I could make or design things.

Selection #6

I am a "people person." It's easy for me to make new friends. I am good at helping friends and family members through difficult times. I prefer team games and sports. I am good at teaching other people things that I enjoy doing. I find it easy to read another person's mood. I'm open to another person's point of view. When I have a problem, I seek out others for advice. I like to get involved with organizing social activities connected to my work, school, religious group, or community. I'd enjoy a career where I could work in close contact with others.

Selection #7

I like to think about my life—what I've done, what I'm doing now, and what I'd like to do in the future. I set goals for myself. I usually make the right choices for myself. I feel as if I could write a self-help book. I enjoy keeping a personal journal. When I have to make a big decision, I tend to trust my own judgment. I am the type of person who is likely to state my opinion even if others around me disagree. When I am in a bad mood, I know what caused it and how to get myself out of it. I'd rather have a job where I can be my own boss or make a lot of my own decisions.

Selection #8

I feel at home in the out-of-doors. I'm aware of changes in the weather and sometimes sense them before they happen. I can recognize different kinds of birds when they come to the bird feeder. I enjoy pets, as well as other kinds of animals. I have a knack for nurturing and growing things. I enjoy working in the garden. I could show you some constellations in the night sky. I often take comfort in the environment and nature. I enjoy finding patterns, relationships, and connections in nature. I like to sort and classify objects. When I was a child, I enjoyed collecting things like stamps or insects or stickers. In fact, I still like to collect things. I think I would prefer a job where I could work with some aspect of nature.

Figure 2.7. AMI Survey Responses

Name: _____

Use this sheet to record your responses to each selection. Do not labor over your response. Remember, there are no right or wrong answers.

Selection #1   These statements describe me

      Very much   A lot   Somewhat   Just a little   Hardly at all

Selection #2   These statements describe me

      Very much   A lot   Somewhat   Just a little   Hardly at all

Selection #3   These statements describe me

      Very much   A lot   Somewhat   Just a little   Hardly at all

Selection #4   These statements describe me

      Very much   A lot   Somewhat   Just a little   Hardly at all

Selection #5   These statements describe me

      Very much   A lot   Somewhat   Just a little   Hardly at all

Selection #6   These statements describe me

      Very much   A lot   Somewhat   Just a little   Hardly at all

Selection #7   These statements describe me

      Very much   A lot   Somewhat   Just a little   Hardly at all

Selection #8   These statements describe me

      Very much   A lot   Somewhat   Just a little   Hardly at all

Figure 2.8. MI Profile Bar Graph

Name_____

	Adult Multiple Intelligences Profile							
Very Much								
A Lot								
Somewhat								
Just a Little								
Hardly at All								
	#1 Music Smart	#2 Body Smart	#3 Word Smart	#4 Math/ Logic Smart	#5 Picture Smart	#6 People Smart	#7 Self Smart	#8 Nature Smart

House-building Activity: This New House

The house-building activity was used as a team-building activity in the AMI project. The different ways in which people approach the activity can be used to stimulate discussion about MI theory. Each of us brings our own strengths to any task we complete. During this activity individual strengths seem to emerge in a natural way.

Materials   A generous quantity of old newspapers Several rolls of masking tape, ruler (to measure length of tape)

The Activity

Have the participants count off to form groups of five or six. Arrange to have someone serve as an impartial observer for each group. This person's job is to keep a running record of what goes on as each group attempts to complete the following task.

Using only sheets of newspaper and masking tape, your group is to construct a house large enough so that at least one person in your group can sit inside it. The house must be able to stand on its own without any additional support. You have 30 minutes to complete this task. Keep track of your expenses as you work. The cost of the materials used during the construction of the house should be calculated using the following information:

Each sheet of newspaper costs $5.00.
Each inch of tape costs $1.00.

Explain that this is a team competition. To win, a group must not only complete its house within the allotted time but also construct the house for the lowest cost. Upon finishing, each group should display the cost of the house somewhere on the exterior of the structure. Tell the groups that they must be able to substantiate how they kept track of their expenses.

Have each group present its house to the other groups. The recorder/observer should also offer a debriefing of the group's experience at this time. After determining which group has won the grand prize, you can also present other awards, such as "most spacious," "most creative," "most unusual," "most likely to withstand an earthquake."

Have the participants reconvene as a large group. Ask them to think about who did the math in each group, who designed the structure, who simply watched and kept everyone's spirits up, who designed the house on paper first, who made sure everyone stayed on task, and who kept track of how much time had elapsed. Discuss how individual intelligence strengths may have influenced the group dynamic as the participants worked on this task.

Activities for Learning About Our Ways of Learning

Photo Journals

Terri Coustan used photographs of students in action to encourage them to discuss their intelligence strengths. This approach works best if the lesson or unit includes a variety of learning activities.

Have students select one or more learning activities the class is doing. Take photographs of the students as they are engaged in the activities they have chosen. Present each student with one or more photos. Have the students either write or talk about why they chose to do the activities depicted in the photos. Connect their responses to the activity and the related intelligences. (See Terri's lessons Coming to America I and Indoor Gardening in Chapter 4.)

How Do I Learn Best?

Diane Paxton built her ESOL students' metacognitive knowledge about their learning preferences with this activity. Diane interviewed her ESOL students at the beginning of the semester to elicit student reflections on their learning preferences. This survey was mainly in the form of pictures, with minimal words. The student circled the picture that most closely portrayed his or her idea in response to these questions.

o   How do I learn best? What kinds of classroom activities help me to learn the most?

o   What is a good ESOL class?

Twice during the semester, Diane conducted a group evaluation of the students' impressions of the topics, activities, processes, and products. At that time, they reviewed specific learning activities, work sheets, and projects the class had done, and students expressed their opinions regarding what helped them to learn the most or the least.

Diane also asked students about their awareness of their own intelligences and about the relationship between their intelligences, the classroom activities, and learning. She then completed a chart with information on each student's responses. This chart was posted on the classroom wall and referred to in subsequent sessions.

Chapter 2 Reflection and Discussion Questions

o   What are your intelligence strengths?

o   How do you think they play out in the ways you teach and learn?

o   How can you observe your students' intelligence strengths?

o   What goals do you have for doing MI Reflections? Why?

o   How might you go about pursuing these goals?

o   What would you anticipate to be the biggest stumbling blocks? How could you get around them?

Chapter 3: MI-INSPIRED INSTRUCTION

The AMI Experience

Introduction

A group of Latino elders is gathered in the kitchen of Centro Hispano in Chelsea, Massachusetts, for their ESOL lesson. One woman scrapes the gelatin from an aloe vera plant while a man blends three chopped onions and water. Another señora chops limes while several others assist and observe her. They are speaking animatedly in halting English, peppered with Spanish, about different natural remedies for various ailments. Their teacher, Diane Paxton, takes photographs that she will later ask her students to sequence. The photos will also serve as a memory prompt when the elders write down their recipes. Later, when the class is doing its customary assessment of the preceding month's activities, several students echo a classmate's sentiments about this activity, "Very good, we learned a lot of words. I'd heard the word blender, *but didn't know what it meant." Another student holds a copy of* Natural Medicines, *the book the group has written as a class project, saying, "This is our literature."*

Several hours' drive north of Chelsea's urban surroundings is Manchester, Vermont, a rural community where another group of adults is hunched over multicolored flash cards and math manipulatives spread out on the table. "Converting measurements" is the topic of this evening's GED/Adult Diploma preparation class, and on each card is a unit of measurement expressed in fraction, percentage, or decimal form. The students' task is to figure out which of the units are equal. There is a lot of laughter and negotiation over correct answers. Meanwhile, Meg Costanzo, their teacher, looks on quietly.

What Is MI-informed Instruction?

MI researchers often refer to MI theory as a lens through which teachers can view and understand their students and their approaches to teaching and learning. Perceiving students through the proverbial MI lens adds detail and depth to teachers' knowledge of who their students are and what they bring to the classroom. Looking at teaching and learning through an MI lens suggests analyzing instructional practices with an eye toward the available range of learning opportunities across areas of students' intelligences and preferences. MI theory validates multisensory, real world–based teaching practices. It is also a tool for developing this broader range of learning opportunities.

In short, MI theory is a "frame of mind" that informs, rather than prescribes, instruction and assessment. The authors use "MI-informed," "MI-based," "MI-inspired," and being "in the spirit of MI theory" interchangeably, to refer to instruction or assessment that takes into account the theory of multiple intelligences in its design and implementation. MI-informed instructional practices are distinct from MI Reflections (MIR) activities, which refer to introducing MI theory explicitly to students and using it as a tool for self-reflection and self-awareness (see Chapter 2).

The two preceding vignettes present distinct examples of MI-informed instruction. In the first example, Diane uses MI theory to enhance the group's health unit. In the second, Meg Costanzo uses MI to create a more engaging, interactive context for math review. As suggested by these two examples, the overall AMI Study experience reiterates the notion that there is no one way to apply MI theory in instruction. Depending on the individual context and goals, as well as each teacher's own take on MI theory, a tremendous variety of MI-informed practices has emerged. At the same time, the AMI Study codirectors have identified several common features of MI-informed teaching and learning in adult learning settings. In the following section, we present these features and share related examples of practice as we identified them in the AMI Study.

Features of MI-informed Practice: Insights From the AMI Classrooms

The common features AMI Study codirectors identified across the many MI-informed approaches and activities developed in the AMI Study can be divided into two categories: 1) features that grow directly out of MI theory; and 2) features that are best described as supportive of, sometimes essential to, the success of MI-informed instructional approaches. For example, we found that MI theory usually translates into offering a variety of diverse learning activities. We can safely assume that this feature draws on a major MI tenet that there exist 8 (or 9) intelligences in which all individuals have potential (see Chapter 1 for descriptions of each intelligence). In other words, that there exists a plurality of intelligences directly suggests that more intelligences should be accounted for in the classroom. A common strategy to which teachers turn to address this aspect of MI theory is, logically, to offer a greater variety of learning activities to their students.

A feature such as "teacher persistence "—teachers' persisting with MI-informed approaches in the face of student resistance—is not drawn directly from the theory. In other words, nothing about MI theory per se suggests or even relates to teacher persistence. Yet, in the context of adult education, where students' resistance to new methods is perhaps the rule rather than the exception, teacher persistence becomes a necessary supportive feature of MI-informed teaching.

Listed here are the most salient features of MI-informed instruction that we identified across the AMI Study classrooms as part of our research findings. A fuller discussion of them follows.

- o   Using MI theory leads teachers to offer a greater variety of learning activities.

- o   The most engaging MI-based lessons make use of content and approaches that are meaningful to students.

- o   MI-based approaches advance learning goals.

- o   Implementing MI-informed practices involves teachers' taking risks.

- o   Persistence pays off with MI-based instruction.

- o   MI-informed learning activities increase student initiative and control over the content or direction of the activities.

- o   Building trust and community in the classroom supports MI-based instruction.

Using MI Theory Leads Teachers to Offer a Greater Variety of Learning Activities

Perhaps the most generative of MI theory's major tenets, that there exists a plurality of intelligences, results in the most common MI-informed practice: providing a greater variety of entry points or ways to engage in a topic or skill area. What this means varies from teacher to teacher. For one teacher, applying MI theory may begin with adding more visual aids, whereas for another teacher, it may mean initiating an interdisciplinary learning project.

For Diane Paxton, MI theory is "only one aspect that I draw on under the umbrella of my teaching" (Kallenbach & Viens, 2001, p. 172). She used MI theory to develop and enhance thematic units and group projects, building on her considerable repertoire of ESOL teaching strategies that already draw on students' multiple intelligences, such as Total Physical Response, jazz chants, and sequencing pictures with text. Diane noted that "MI also helped to overcome the problem of various levels in the class, helping to ensure language acquisition opportunities for all students" (Paxton, 1998). For AMI Sourcebook pilot teacher Carol Beima it meant that she "learned the value of leaving some assignments more open-ended and seeing the multiple ways [they] may be completed" (Beima, 1999).

Giving students intelligences-based choices among learning and assessment activities is a common way teachers deliver a variety of learning activities to their students. Lesson formats that gave students choices that corresponded loosely to the eight intelligences became especially popular among AMI teachers. Martha Jean's Choose 3 activities gave students nine or ten activity options from which to choose to work in GED topic areas. These choice-based activities were typically followed by exercises in GED workbooks. Lezlie Rocka had her students preview and review readings in her basic literacy class with choice-based pre- and postreading activities. For example, after reading a chapter in *Meet Addy*, about a teen-age girl born into slavery who escapes with her mother to freedom, students could draw a picture representing a scene, act out a scene, make a map of Addy's journey, or pick a song that would give inspiration on such a journey, among other options.

Dianne Marlowe implemented an interdisciplinary learning project in her GED class that combined instruction in language arts and math and was bolstered by ongoing, written student reflections. A series of small-group, paper-and-pencil math activities on tangrams from *Multiple Intelligences in the Math Classroom* (Martin, 1996) led the way to increasingly more hands-on activities with geometric shapes. The geometry unit culminated in a quilting project. To build students' interest in the project and to develop their reading and writing skills, Dianne had the class read poetry and essays about quilts and watch a video on the subject. She also made available picture books of quilts and hung a poster of a quilt in front of the classroom for inspiration and focus. The unit culminated with the group's sewing together the quilt squares each student had designed and made to form a large class quilt.

In Dianne Marlowe's class, as well as in every other AMI class, MI-based activities complemented more traditional lessons and direct instruction on discrete skills. For example, work sheets and quizzes from the GED text reinforced the geometry content during the quilting project. Sometimes an MI-based activity functioned as a hook that got students engaged and more willing to grapple with more abstract, rote, or decontextualized material. This was especially true in GED classes. As well, teachers gave students the option of working in more traditional formats, such as work sheets, if the given MI-based activity did not appeal to them. Meg Costanzo found that her concern that most students would go for the "quick fix" work sheets when given the choice turned out to be unfounded. She theorized, "Our class discussions about MI theory and the students' perception of my willingness to respect and honor the varied intelligences that they demonstrate have made them more receptive to alternative types of teaching" (Costanzo, 1997a).

Several AMI teachers concluded that MI theory gave them license and a sound rationale to be more playful and creative with their teaching and to include activities that might otherwise appear too juvenile or entertaining. Martha Jean's students repeatedly referred to "having fun while learning" as a central reason why her MI-informed approach helped them prepare for the GED (Kallenbach & Viens, 2001, p. 113). Her students noted that her Choose 3 format engaged them and kept them interested. Their responses were validated by increased attendance compared to that in her non-MI-informed GED class and fewer student task-avoidance behaviors, such as asking for coffee and cigarette breaks and engaging in off-topic conversations or off-task use of activity materials.

Whether or not playfulness and fun were a part of the teaching goal, students experienced many MI-informed activities as such. These included many real world activities like gardening, designing student recruitment strategies, writing and illustrating instructions for home remedies, and even calculating attendance rates. Almost without exception, in classrooms that changed from individual to more group work in the course of the AMI Study, students commented on how much they enjoyed being able to interact with peers and learn from them.

The Most Engaging MI-based Lessons Use Content and Approaches That Are Meaningful to Students

MI theory defines intelligence as manifesting itself in the problems people solve and the products they make. Thus approaches that invite students to construct their own meaning and understanding through authentic problem-solving and their intelligence strengths are directly implied by MI theory. More than that, using real world applications of MI theory proves more meaningful to students.

The AMI experience validates the theories and practices that give primacy to authentic learning that is meaningful to students and connects to their lives. The MI-based lessons that were the most favored by students, and noted by teachers for high student engagement, were ones where the content reflected student interests and realities. The best were the lessons that also offered an authentic audience and an opportunity for students to make a difference.

Betsy Cornwell concluded that "many of the MI-based authentic tasks I tried seemed to very effectively create a safe, playful learning environment" (Kallenbach & Viens, 2001, p. 24). She and her colleagues found some MI-based activities more authentic than others. She and another AMI teacher who did a math activity where students measured the length of a million dollar bills placed one after another found it did not engage the students. Measuring the length of a million dollars may be an MI-based activity, but it is probably not meaningful to low-income adults, whereas doing comparison activities with food students use and can eat afterward had greater relevance and appeal.

Although Betsy's goal of helping her students become more independent learners did not change, the ways in which she aligned this goal with her teaching practice did change considerably, and to good effect. She made progress toward her goal when she began to connect her student Debbie's interests to MI-based activities. Observing that Debbie was genuinely interested in people, Betsy found ways to tap into that interest. Likewise, when Debbie wrote about her experience with sexual abuse for a newsletter, she became motivated for the first time to edit her own writing.

For Diane Paxton's students, it was creating their book *Natural Medicines,* representing their own knowledge on the subject, that sustained their interest longer than other learning activities. Diane writes,

> We spent almost two months on the Natural Medicines book, photographing, talking, writing, editing, drawing, and making the recipes, and they were not bored at all.... Even more significant was that when the book was finished, and the students read their pieces from the

> book out loud, they all listened to each other. They still demonstrated high interest by actually asking questions of each other after the readings. This kind of questioning at their own instigation was unprecedented with this group. (Paxton, 1997)

Meg Costanzo's students rated as their favorite the project to devise ways to increase enrollment in their learning center. They redesigned the center's recruitment flyer and sign outside the building. They wrote a public service announcement, interviewed program graduates, and calculated attendance rates. Meg comments,

> I did not even have to ask the students to turn in their assignments. Three students had their work out and ready to turn in before I even brought up the subject.... The students are taking their work on this project seriously. This underscores the value of assigning work that is authentic and meaningful to students. (Costanzo, 1997a)

The AMI experience confirms that having an authentic audience and a topic that students consider relevant or important are the foundation pieces of a lesson that engages students. When the lesson's design also invites students to use their multiple intelligences, it has the ingredients for a successful learning experience.

MI-based Approaches Advance Learning Goals

As a theory of intelligence, MI describes in what ways people process information and engage with their world. In the classroom, MI theory is a means to attain learning goals; the intelligences should not become the learning goals themselves (see Chapter 1). MI practices that are truly in the spirit of MI are developed with learning goals in mind, like preparing for a GED test, learning to write an essay, or learning to converse in English. Disparate activities like singing songs or cooking meals together to "get in" intelligences with no attention paid to the overall course goals should not be characterized as MI-based instruction.

The learning goals in the AMI classrooms were much the same as those in any ESOL, reading/writing, math, or GED class. These goals did not change, but the AMI teachers found ways to use the intelligences as a guide to develop or adapt existing learning activities to help students reach learning goals. They engaged in more spatial activities, ranging from using photographs as writing prompts to creating collages or building with Play-Doh®. They sought ways to integrate more options for movement into the lessons. They drew on their students' naturalist intelligences through ecology content. Many AMI ABE/GED teachers struggled with how they could use music effectively in their lessons, whereas the ESOL teachers were more accustomed to integrating lyrics and singing into language learning.

Implementing MI-informed Practices Involves Teachers' Taking Risks

The AMI teachers discovered, much to their relief, that they themselves did not have to excel in all intelligence areas; however, they did have to venture out, in some respects, into unfamiliar areas of perhaps less comfort. In providing options for students to learn through different types of experiences and media, like music, movement, clay, or pictures, they found that they were rewarded for their courage to move beyond their own MI comfort zone by a higher level of student engagement and output, and by a deepened knowledge of their students. AMI teacher Dianne Marlowe took a risk with her teaching, as she explains:

> The quilting project was for me a really challenging project. I had never quilted before (but thankfully my co-teacher, Esther, had) and this project meant teaching out of my own area of weakness. Secondly, I have always felt very weak in visual/spatial skills. This project has taught me that it is OK and perhaps really good to share some of the feelings and insecurities the students may also have; this keeps me in touch with what it is like to be a learner. (Marlowe, 1997)

All but one of the AMI teachers concluded that MI theory pushed them to take more risks and broaden their teaching beyond what they had been doing. The level of creativity in their lessons increased discernibly. Lezlie Rocka, for example, went from believing that MI theory had little to offer to her already multisensory teaching approach to asserting that MI theory informed and broadened her multi-

sensory approach to teaching reading and writing. The amount of risk-taking that MI-informed instruction calls for is clearly a function of the teacher's existing practices and comfort level with trying something new. Thus, although risk-taking is not part of MI theory per se, many practitioners seemed to feel that applying the theory in education requires it.

Persistence Pays Off With MI-based Instruction

For most teachers and learners, using MI in teaching and learning to its fullest potential requires changing perceptions about effective teaching and learning. It requires actively helping students connect what they know about themselves to the learning at hand. That takes time and persistence. Some students might be well aware that they are good at woodworking, and they might even know that it entails spatial and bodily-kinesthetic intelligences. But connecting that knowledge to how they could improve their math or writing skills in a GED class is another matter altogether.

Helping students translate their knowledge of their intelligence strengths into effective learning strategies takes a lot of prompting and practice. In that process, modeling is the key. As Meg Costanzo states, "Modeling different techniques over and over again will allow students to select the approaches which work best for them" (Costanzo, 1997a). For example, Meg concluded that "webbing," also called mind-mapping, was a useful prewriting technique for some of her spatially talented students.

Meg made it a part of her teaching routine to regularly ask students to identify what intelligences they used in a particular learning activity. In addition, she had students create "personal learning resource books" in which they tracked how they were using their intelligence strengths to learn, kept samples of their writings and individual project work, and reflected on personal and educational goals. Meg asked students to refer to their "personal learning resource books" at the beginning of each class to talk about what was covered in the previous class. This also served as a mechanism to share that information with students who had missed the class.

Meg's persistence with MI-based instruction and related reflections paid off in improved student attendance that increased 220% since the beginning of her involvement in the AMI Study. It also resulted in her students' improved metacognitive and learning strategies.

Dianne Marlowe's quilting project also required a hefty amount of gentle persistence, especially with her male students. She did not let her male students off the hook. In the end, they all praised the project. Dianne writes,

> We modeled, sat with the individuals, helped them, and supported them in getting past the block. The male who resisted cutting and selecting fabric turned out to contribute the most sewing. He sewed the entire backing to the quilt and then chose and put the buttons on to tie it. As the teachers, both Esther and I pushed to make it work. By so doing, it did work. We were open and part of the community of learners. We supported students every step of the way and approached every part of this project with the absolute assumption it would work. Students, in turn, gave their support and energy to this project. (Marlowe, 1997)

MI-informed Learning Activities Increase Student Initiative and Control Over the Content or Direction of the Activities

MI-based classes invite full student participation and give students more control over how they process and demonstrate their learning. When teachers give students choices in how they learn and demonstrate what they have learned, they are effectively giving some control to students. It is possible that the act of validating students' strengths, interests, and preferences is an important first step that helps build the students' self-confidence and enables them to take control over their own learning and the curriculum. Furthermore, when students examine their strengths, they are likely to deepen their self-knowledge, which gives them a firmer foundation from which to direct their learning.

The AMI teachers perceived a noticeable shift in the teacher-to-student power relations as a result of their MI-based practices. Over time, as students experienced diverse MI-based learning activities, they began taking more initiative and control over the content or direction of the activities.

Several AMI teachers found themselves relinquishing some control by virtue of giving students choices and respecting their individual ways of learning and knowing. Terri Coustan found that, as students began to express preferences through choice-based activities, they also became more assertive in other ways, shifting the balance of power in the classroom somewhat. She writes,

> My experience over the past few years had shown me that these students were reluctant to share their preferences with me. I had almost given up hope of ever being able to learn their preferences and had decided that this behavior was related to learners with limited English. Now, the students appeared to have reached a benchmark or milestone.... More students made choices. And those choices reflected both what the students liked and did not like about the activities I suggested. (Coustan, 1998)

Likewise, Lezlie Rocka comments, "My class became more interactive and student-directed as I experimented with MI theory. Before this research project, I did most of the leading and dictated the order of the activities" (Kallenbach & Viens, 2001, p. 214). Sharing power with students was an unanticipated outcome of the changes Terri and Lezlie made in their teaching.

Exploring how MI theory might serve to empower students was the focus of Wendy Quiñones's research project. Her answer was "yes" in terms of the classroom-based power relations. She reported,

> A change in the teacher–student relationship in the classroom rapidly became apparent. The combination of assignments based on multiple intelligences with the strategy of allowing students to choose their own assignments was the best I have yet found for sharing power while giving students a firm structure within which to work. (Kallenbach & Viens, 2001, p. 190)

In Meg Costanzo's GED class, the students decided to vote among the different options they had come up with for how to respond to Meg's question, "What can we do, as a class, to make the Tutorial Center a more comfortable environment in which to work and learn?" She reports that the students were initially baffled and amused when she told them that it was their project and they were to decide on the best course(s) of action. They soon developed complete ownership over this mini-project, generated possible courses of action, and implemented the one they chose.

Even when the MI-based activity does not entail choices, but encourages group work, students begin to look to each other as sources of knowledge and ideas. Given encouragement from the teacher and challenging learning projects, they look less to the teacher for information and direction at every step. Jean Mantzaris's class is a good example of this. Jean's lessons did not have a Choose 3 format, but they allowed for different entry points, as in the Memory Lane activity and "Jobopoly" game. Jean writes,

> Once I started to diversify my lesson plans, I began to look to the students for more input. . . . As time went on students took over decision-making for activities such as the career board game. For example, they wrote all the "Chance" cards for the game. Their ideas were quite different from mine in that they focused more on the kinds of assistance they would need, whereas I would have included some luxury items such as a trip to a warm island, a new car, jewelry, etc. They added two new squares: on-the-job training and Ph.D. programs. They developed the MI "show" for teachers on their own. I became a guide and participant in these activities designed by the students. As one of my students commented, "It was a lot of fun and showed how much fun a bunch of people could accomplish if they got together." (Kallenbach & Viens, 2001, p. 142)

A shift in the balance of power in the classroom changes the classroom dynamic and requires teachers and students to renegotiate their roles. Teachers need to resist the urge to provide all answers and solutions while creating enough structure for learning. Students need to look more to themselves and each other for ideas and direction when given the opportunity. As does any significant change in belief and practice, it takes time and persistence.

Building Trust and Community in the Classroom Supports MI-based Instruction

Several AMI teachers found that building trust and community in the classroom is necessary for MI-based instruction to be embraced by most students. It is trust and mutual respect that enable people to take risks into the unfamiliar together, to perform a skit, to tell a story, to build something, or to make a drawing. AMI teacher Diane Paxton comments,

> For both my groups of students, the change in perceptions took time, so that they could bond together as a class, and develop trust in me as their teacher. Trust developed and helped change perceptions because they saw that even though what I was doing in the class did not look like it was in their best interests, they saw over time that it was. (Paxton, 1998)

Although giving students time to get to know each other and the teacher and easing them into nontraditional learning activities is one way to build trust in the classroom, there are various ways in which teachers can aid this process. One way is to get people working together on learning activities. AMI Sourcebook pilot teacher Carol Beima reports,

> The directed interpersonal and hands-on activities seemed to help the new students become actively involved more easily than in previous quarters. There was conversation about the work and laughter as students supported and encouraged the efforts of their classmates. As class has continued, I feel that the bond formed by the interpersonal activities has made it easier for some students to risk explaining a math solution or sharing personal writing at an earlier stage in the quarter. This connection to others may be a factor in better student attendance, as I usually have over 70% of students attending regularly. (Beima, 1999a)

Another way is to implement activities that have as their explicit goal community building. Dianne Marlowe had students work in groups to build a house out of newspaper with the requirement that a person had to fit inside it. Several students later did the same activity with their children (see House-building Activity in Chapter 2).

Yet another avenue to help students feel at ease with nontraditional learning activities and with one another is to create opportunities for people to get to know each other's interests and strengths. Activities such as Meg Costanzo's "Something I Do Well" writing assignment followed by student sharing serve that purpose, as do other MIR activities when they are shared in the group. Meg notes, "It is hard for new students to feel comfortable sharing personal ideas in a strange setting. I made certain that the two new women in class did not feel pressured to respond to this assignment [to make a talisman]. Again, the importance of building up a feeling of trust is underscored" (Costanzo, 1997b).

Conclusion

The authors' goal for this chapter was to offer some guidance and ideas culled from the AMI Study for teachers who are considering or initiating MI-informed instruction. We have found MI-informed instructional practices to consist of a multitude of "translations," set in the context of several common, underlying features introduced in this chapter. Using MI theory as a tool for developing teaching and learning activities can be liberating in that it allows teachers to express their individual styles and creativity, and tap their own intelligence strengths. On the other hand, it also can be challenging in that prescriptive strategies are far more straightforward to implement. Implementing MI-informed teaching and learning approaches means interpreting MI theory and identifying appropriate applications for one's own setting. Honoring the pluralistic nature of intelligence, persisting in the face of student resistance, taking risks in the classroom, and giving up control to students are a lot harder than implementing a particular strategy.

AMI teachers found that using content that is authentic and meaningful to students, being creatively and kindly persistent, and building community and trust in the learning group are all key elements to successful MI implementation. Moreover, they found their efforts well rewarded. In particular, they found that MI-informed strategies, especially student choice, led to their students' taking more control over their learning and developing their own voices. As students rose to the challenge, teachers and students shifted their paradigm of not only what is desirable but also what is possible. As one of the AMI teachers said about MI theory in education: "In the end, it's about looking at everyone from a strengths perspective. We all have strengths."

Two AMI Teachers' Perspectives: Planning Curriculum With MI Theory

Introduction

Terri and Lezlie used MI theory to make classroom learning experiences more likely to speak to all their students' strengths and interests. Terri worked with ESOL students, most of whom were not literate in their native language. Lezlie taught primarily native English-speaking, beginning literacy students. They offered their students a more diverse blend of activities that they felt reflected their students' particular strengths and preferred learning strategies.

Terri Coustan

I began applying MI theory by observing students and articulating those observations as demonstrations of certain intelligences. By gathering my observations, I was able to identify informally individual students' strengths and interests. Observing students and integrating new knowledge of their strengths is an iterative process: I observed students' participation in class, which in turn informed my planning process. When students did particular things well and made consistent choices as to the kinds of activities they preferred, I could see a pattern emerge for each student.

For example, after he became comfortable with the Choose 3 Activities format I used, Choua often selected activities in which he could use his hands to make objects, such as a wooden truck. Lor chose activities that involved logical-mathematical processes, such as calendar or computer tasks. These examples were consistent with activities they chose on other days as well, such as Lor's counting the number of students present.

Although these students did not work exclusively in any one domain, they seemed to be drawn, especially initially, to domains that reflected specific intelligences. I then wove this information into my future lesson plans. I also tried to include many points of entry into the activities: visual (pictures), sequencing, personal experiences, hands-on activities, and real-life experiences.

Applying MI theory does not necessarily imply an overhaul of one's curriculum. Nor does it suggest abandoning activities that are important to you or your class. I found it made the most sense to apply MI theory to what I was already doing. I started in one subject and expanded as I felt the need or opportunity to do so. As more of my students' intelligences were revealed to me, I tried to link more options into my curricula for students to express and use their strengths. For me, the key to teaching "à la MI" is wearing those MI "lenses."

Lezlie Rocka

I was focusing on writing instruction when I began this project. I observed that my students learned a lot about writing by teaching each other how to write, so I incorporated peer-teaching experiences into the lessons. This type of practice is neither new nor unique to MI theory. From an MI-informed perspective, I thought of peer teaching as tapping into my students' interpersonal intelligence. I then considered other ways to engage my students' interpersonal strengths. For example, I added dramatic presentations to the postreading options I gave to students.

Before the AMI Study, my teaching was very much informed by a multisensory approach. That is, I used strategies to get students to use as many senses as possible in their learning. Rather than replace my multisensory approach with one based on MI, it made perfect sense to use multisensory lessons as a starting point.

My *Meet Addy* lesson plan demonstrates how I took a multisensory reading lesson and enhanced it by applying MI theory (see Activities to Inspire Reading for Meaning in Chapter 4). *Meet Addy* is historical fiction about the experiences of slaves escaping captivity via the Underground Railroad. Addy is a young teenage girl who escapes with her mother to freedom. I began with a whole-group prereading exercise and then asked students to take turns reading the text aloud. While they read, I coached them in applying all the multisensory skills they had already learned, including using their finger, a pencil, or a

bookmark to help guide their eyes; focusing on beginning or ending sounds of words; discussing every paragraph; defining and discussing new words; and using mnemonic devices.

Revisiting the lesson from an MI perspective, I enhanced the postreading activities, adding a set of experiences from which my students could choose, such as drawing something from the reading, making a map, or acting out a scene. These activities were meant to enhance students' understanding of the reading and to give them options through which to express their understanding. In coming up with the options, I drew on my observations of the types of activities students enjoyed and in which they seemed to do well.

These diverse postreading experiences gave students choices in how they demonstrated their learning. Because giving my students choices emerged as a powerful teaching strategy in my classroom, I termed it "choice expression." I made sure to integrate some kind of student choice expression every time we read in class. I varied the choices, always trying to include a range so as to allow students the opportunity to process the reading and demonstrate their knowledge using their different intelligence strengths.

MI-based activities seemed to facilitate my students' learning. For example, I observed that students struggled more with reading comprehension when they only read and wrote to understand it. Students seemed to gain a better understanding of a story when given the opportunity to choose among intelligences-based options on how they would express that understanding. This seemed to help them make more meaning out of the text and to remember the story better. While students were doing their reading-related projects, they combed through the stories to get information that was more specific. They wanted to be sure their projects were accurate and detailed, in contrast to the familiar attitude of just wanting to get the report done. Reading became a tool to do the projects. Whereas a book report makes the reading the end, in this case reading became the means to the end. The more students expressed and explored meaning in their own ways, the more I was surprised and sometimes moved by the depth of their responses.

Chapter 3 Reflection and Discussion Questions

o   How do your teaching experiences compare with those of the AMI teachers discussed in this chapter?

o   How do you currently draw on your students' particular strengths in your teaching?

o   How do you determine which content or teaching strategies are meaningful to your students?

o   What do you currently do to build trust and community in your classroom?

o   Can you think of ways to further diversify your teaching strategies that would be in keeping with your goals for the class?

o   What needs to be in place in order for you to try out these MI-based teaching strategies (materials, space, your comfort zone, etc.)?

Chapter 4: MI-INSPIRED LESSONS

What's MI About These Lessons?

The Adult Multiple Intelligences (AMI) Study teachers developed all the lessons and lesson formats in this section during their participation in the AMI Study. MI theory provided the impetus for several AMI teachers to develop new teaching approaches. Perhaps the best example of this is the Choose 3 lesson format which gives students the opportunity to choose how they will work on a topic or skill among several MI-based options. The MI-inspired thematic units incorporate several intelligences and provide multiple ways for students to explore and learn topics and skills.

MI theory also prompted AMI teachers to identify existing techniques or tools that helped students tap into a greater variety of intelligences. Regardless of how commonplace the technique, it was intentionally chosen by the teacher as one way to apply MI theory. For example, Wendy Quiñones's Parts of Speech Trading Game lesson stays true to its objective of teaching the parts of speech while incorporating an interpersonal and a hands-on, bodily-kinesthetic dimension. Likewise, many of the math lessons teachers developed under the AMI umbrella incorporate manipulatives, such as beans and small figures. Clearly, math manipulatives did not evolve from MI theory itself. Rather, MI theory led teachers to math manipulatives. Their drive to incorporate different intelligences into the classroom led them to add math manipulatives to their repertoire. Indeed, for two out of the four AMI teachers who taught math, manipulatives were a new and somewhat intimidating teaching tool. What for one teacher is "old hat" is a devel-opmental leap for another. An MI framework provided a theoretical bridge for these teachers.

MI theory provided a rationale and basis for the development of each of the lessons in this chapter. Reflecting the primary course objectives of either reading and writing or math, linguistic or logical-mathematical intelligences figure prominently in many of these lessons. What makes them different is that each lesson has an "MI twist," incorporating teaching techniques or approaches that draw on more than the intelligences typically used to teach any given curriculum objective.

Guidelines for Planning MI-informed Lessons

1. List the curriculum objective for this lesson, as well as content and skills to be covered.

2. Consider and list your students' talents and interests inside and outside of the classroom that could inform the lesson. In particular, note the interests and talents of those students you feel are hard to reach, who don't seem to be engaged, and/or who need specific help in the subject or skill covered by this lesson.

3. Generate a list of activities that fit the lesson's objectives and that either engage a range of talents and interests or target a particular student's talents and interests. That is, activities can be developed based on a range of domains (loosely based on the eight intelligences) that are or are not specifically related to your students' proclivities.

    o   Brainstorm lesson activities that directly or indirectly tap into students' talents and interests when you introduce new concepts or skills;

    o   at the practice stage; and/or,

    o   when students demonstrate their understanding.

If, for example, you know your student is a car mechanic, it is probably safe to assume that he has an interest in cars, is good with his hands, and likes to fix things. Can some aspect of the topic of cars and their attributes be woven into the lesson or a preactivity? What part of the lesson could be hands-on to tap this student's likely fine motor ability?

4. What are some corresponding real world activities that would be appropriate and meaningful for the lesson(s)?

5. Review your list of activities and note the intelligences that have been tapped. Are there intelligence areas that you have not included because you do not feel comfortable or competent enough to develop or implement related activities? Can you invite a colleague to coteach or help you include these areas?

6. Consider offering your students a choice or choices among activities. Creating choices is also an effective way to allow for activities in areas in which you personally do not feel comfortable. At what stage(s) (introduction, practice stage, assessment) will choice be offered?

7. Finalize your lesson plan and activities. List materials needed for the activity(ies).

8. You may want to plan an explanation about MI and about how everyone learns differently or a trust-building preactivity to ease them into this lesson.

MI Lesson Formats

— Choose 3 Lesson Format —

Martha Jean

Martha Jean found this lesson format popular with her adult students because it allowed them to choose how they wanted to learn or review the subject matter at hand.

Subject   Applicable to all subject areas
Time   Between 1 hour and $1^1/_2$ hours, once a week

Background

Because I work with GED preparation classes, I am frequently frustrated by the narrowness of the curriculum I must teach. I wanted to find a way to expand the number of learning activities that my students could experience while still preparing for the five exams they need to pass in order to earn their equivalency diplomas. I was especially concerned with helping those students who experience learning disabilities (LD) and/or attention deficit disorders (ADD or ADHD) meet with success in our program. I came up with a format that I call Choose 3, wherein the students can select how to practice or review the material we have studied in class by completing three related MI-inspired activities from specific lists I have developed for each lesson. Choose 3 lessons are designed so that the learner will apply learning (in any subject) in at least three different ways, using different strengths or intelligences to better understand and remember the idea.

On the days I use this format, I hand out the Choose 3 activity page and we read it aloud as a class. My students can ask questions and get clarification before they begin. Students are reminded that they can work alone, with a teammate, or in a group. I give enough time for everyone to do three of the choices. If someone finishes before the time is up, he or she can do another activity from Choose 3 or complete other class work until everyone has finished. When everyone has completed the three choices, the students gather around the table to share which choices they have made, and, if they are willing, show the class what they did. This serves as yet another review as students listen to each other's ideas.

Below is a sample Choose 3 lesson. More Choose 3 lessons are found in the sections that follow.

Perimeter, Area, and Volume

Subject   Math
Curriculum Objective
         To review the concepts of perimeter, area, and volume
Materials   Markers, paint, Play-Doh®, keyboard, measuring tape, pen, paper

The Lesson

Words to remember:

Perimeter: rim, edge
Area: surface (surface area)
Volume: how much it will hold

Use the formula page found in the GED workbook to help you with these activities.
1.   Using markers, paint, or Play-Doh®, show the perimeter of a square, the area of a triangle, and the volume of a tube (long, circular-shaped solid figure)
2.   Create a tune on the keyboard or write a song or a chant that describes perimeter, area, and volume.
3.   Measure the perimeter of the classroom, figure out the area of the floor, and calculate or approximate the volume of air in the classroom.

4.   You just won a TV, a swimming pool, a coffee maker, a car, curtains, and a set of pans. You need to know if they will fit in the places you want to put them in your house, yard, or garage.

   a.   List five things you might use to find the perimeter.

   b.   List five things you might use to find the area.

   c.   List five items you might use to find the volume.

5.   For each different measure, brainstorm at least three different ways that you could figure out the perimeter and area of your outlined body and the volume of your whole body.

Reflections and Student Responses

I found this lesson format to be very successful, especially for students who have difficulty learning. Not only did the attendance of LD and/or ADD/ADHD students improve when lessons were presented this way but also their progress toward GED readiness increased. I found that the students needed fewer explanations about the material being studied when they were given the opportunity to choose how they wanted to go about learning it. Additionally, my students reported enjoying these kinds of lessons. There always seemed to be a choice that the learner felt comfortable trying either alone or with a partner. The students were more willing to start the class and do the workbook activities. There was much less avoidance by way of classroom disruptions, repeated requests for cigarette or coffee breaks, or decisions to go home early. My own experiences as well as the students' words and actions repeatedly showed me that they wanted to use their intelligence strengths to understand and review what they needed to learn.

The following quotes typify the types of comments that I frequently heard from students after they had worked on Choose 3 activities.

> These [activities] give you a different way of looking at problems. You go through the problem more this way. In the workbook you just do the problem, that's it, and this you can work together.

When I asked this student how doing the workbook exclusively would have affected her progress, she replied,

> I'd probably still [working] be on the math in the beginning. I concentrate more with those [Choose 3]. My mind drifts if I just do the workbook.

— Homework Students Love —

Wendy Quiñones

Wendy came up with a list of project possibilities that encourage students to draw upon their strongest intelligences as they design their own homework assignments.

Subject   Varies with each project
Time   Students work on these assignments at home on their own time
Materials Writing paper, drawing paper, art supplies

Background

The majority of my students already have their GEDs or diplomas but are in transition and need both improved academic skills and self-esteem to move successfully into the next phase of their lives. Most have had unsuccessful experiences with standard education and need encouragement to think that they can learn at all—much less learn in a nontraditional way.

The Lesson

I used project-based homework assignments primarily for a weekly women's history class. In 13 weeks, we covered a wide range of topics in class, from the position of women in the Christian religious tradition, to women in the arts, to the history of housework. In addition to their class readings, students took part in class presentations, performances, and MI-based classroom activities centering on these themes.

At the beginning of the course, I passed out a generic list of project possibilities, organized by type of intelligence, and asked students to use this list as a jumping-off point for their homework projects. I emphasized that the list was not exhaustive but merely a source of some potential ideas that might help them generate their own projects. My goal was to encourage them to use their creativity in responding to and working with the material presented that week.

I often found that simply asking students to respond to what they had learned was enough to stimulate them to creative heights. Sometimes, though, I would ask them to solve a particular problem. One week, for example, when we had discussed the traditional Christian representation of a male deity and what effect this might have had on women's self-concept over the centuries, I asked students to represent their ideas of divinity in female form. The range of projects was impressive, from posters to multimedia creations to poetry to original music. Later, after reading a path-breaking historian's description of her experience in trying to bring academic respectability to the discipline of women's history, several students responded with meticulous and beautifully presented timelines of her life. I reserved time during each class for students to present their projects to each other. Some liked to do this and others did not; it was up to them. I kept many of these projects up around the room and documented them in photographs.

Project Possibilities

I derived my generic project list from suggestions in both *The Multiple Intelligences Handbook* by Bruce Campbell (1994) and *Seven Kinds of Smart* by Thomas Armstrong (1993). The list offered just a sampling of the types of activities that the students might want to choose.

Word Smart (Linguistic Intelligence)
o   Tell or write a story or poem about your topic or about something you learned.
o   List and explain memorable things people said about what you learned.
o   Look up the history and derivation of typical or important vocabulary specific to your topic.

Logic Smart [Math Smart] (Logical-Mathematical Intelligence)
o   Make a timeline of events you learned about.
o   Make a flow chart (or other kind of diagram) to show what you learned.

 o Calculate various arithmetic functions having to do with what you learned.

Body Smart (Bodily-Kinesthetic Intelligence)

 o Plan and perform a pantomime about your topic.

 o Describe the physical reactions you had (or didn't have) to your topic.

 o Build or sculpt a representation of what you learned.

Picture Smart (Spatial Intelligence)

 o Draw a picture representing what you learned.

 o Represent your topic as a floor plan, jigsaw puzzle, or three-dimensional model.

 o Describe what you learned as it would appear in a work of art (painting, photograph, drawing, and so on).

 o Make a storyboard for a videotape of your topic.

Music Smart (Musical Intelligence)

 o Write a song or musical composition about what you learned, or just sing a song that describes what you learned.

 o Write new lyrics about your topic that will fit a familiar tune.

 o Sing a song that represents something important about your topic.

 o Put into rhythmic form some important information about concepts, people, or events concerning your topic.

People Smart (Interpersonal Intelligence)

 o Map or describe the personal relationships you learned about.

 o Describe, draw, or otherwise represent the various codes of behavior, styles of dress, appropriate and inappropriate mannerisms, and other nonverbal information important to your topic.

 o Describe how various people you learned about do or do not conform to certain stereotypes.

Self Smart (Intrapersonal Intelligence)

 o Describe or represent how what you learned satisfied (or didn't satisfy) different aspects of yourself.

 o Describe or represent how this topic ties in (or doesn't tie in) with your goals for yourself.

 o Describe or represent the various kinds of emotions your topic produced (or didn't produce) in you.

Reflections and Student Responses

 o Vastly different projects executed with extraordinary skill gave students and me visible, tangible proof of the existence of multiple intelligences. The experience allowed students both to see and to value their differences. Students loved it! "I never thought that I'd say I enjoyed doing my homework, or that it enlivened me, rather than draining me," wrote one student in her evaluation of the class.

 o Project-based homework allowed me to get around the problem of how to teach using my own weak intelligences. By concentrating on the way students learned, and allowing the students to choose their projects, my own weaknesses in math and bodily-kinesthetic did not have to limit my students' opportunities to use those two intelligences in their own learning.

 o Allowing students to choose their own way of presenting what they had learned reinforced my message to students that they are competent learners and decision-makers. Many of my students responded by increasing their responsibility for and commitment to their own learning, as well as their participation in the classroom.

— Putting on Our MI Lenses —

Wendy Quiñones

Wendy found that adding this preactivity component to her lessons enhanced the learning experience for her students.

> The class had read an excerpt from Hansberry's *A Raisin in the Sun.* After we read it, analyzing for the literary terms, I showed them the Danny Glover movie version and only the segment we read.... The most stunning results were with body smart and music smart. The people watching body language were really able to focus on it and learn a lot about what it added to the production. The people listening to the music picked up on the contrast between celebrating music that came to an abrupt end with the foreboding knock on the door. They noticed when there was music and when there was no sound to shade the characters' speech
>
> ~ Judy Hickey, AMI Sourcebook Pilot Teacher, 1999

Background

I prepare my students for certain learning experiences by having them preview a list of related questions. I encourage the students to keep one or two of these questions in mind throughout the activity. I have used this method of helping students organize their learning experiences on a number of occasions, with varying degrees of success. I will describe the two most successful applications—one used with a video and one with a field trip.

I imagine questions like the ones listed on the following pages could be developed for almost any activity a class might undertake. The important thing is to make sure you address at least one question corresponding to each intelligence. The questions should be as varied as you can make them, so students will have a wide spectrum of choices.

Make sure students choose only one or two questions to focus on. Many will want to answer all of them, but this dilutes their concentration. The power of this exercise comes from having students focus narrowly in the area of their strength, and then seeing how those different strengths produce different insights and experiences that enrich everyone's appreciation of the activity.

Also, make sure students understand the vocabulary used in the questions. Several of mine didn't know that a floor plan was an architectural map.

Video Lesson

Materials   Video of *Educating Rita*, VCR and monitor, list of related questions

Educating Rita is a movie about Rita (Julie Walters), a working-class hairdresser with a sharp wit, who is married to Denny, and at 26 doesn't want a baby. She wants to discover herself, so she joins the Open University. Dr. Frank Bryant (Michael Caine) is a disillusioned university professor of literature. His marriage has failed, his girlfriend is having an affair with his best friend, and he can't get through the day without downing a bottle or two of whisky. He refers to himself as an appalling teacher of appalling students. What Frank needs is a challenge–along comes Rita. As Rita's intellectual perspective extends, she becomes torn between her oppressive home life and the attractive, but pretentious, world of her amorous tutor.

The film *Educating Rita* is a wonderful representation of both the growth and the losses that can occur in successful adult education. I recommend it highly for all teachers; in this case, I wanted to use it as a jumping-off point for students to discuss their own experiences. I developed a set of questions about the film, each intended to address a specific intelligence, and handed them out to students before we watched the film. I asked them to choose one or two questions that felt comfortable, that seemed to be things they would normally pay attention to, and to keep them in mind while watching. (*Educating Rita* lends itself nicely to watching in two discrete sections, if your class time requires this, and so can produce either one or two discussions based on the questions.) Here are some sample questions I posed:

1. What are some ways in which you understand at first that Rita doesn't fit in at the university?

2. Does the film have a viewpoint about the life of university people? What are some ways it shows this?

3. What are some ways that the film uses rooms and buildings or inside and outside space to tell things about Rita's life and the changes taking place in it?

4. What are some ways in which Frank and Rita's relationship changes from the beginning to the end of the film?

5. What are some ways in which we know that Rita is changing? What are some ways in which we can tell that she realizes she is changing?

6. What are some ways that Rita's appearance changes through the film? What does this say about her?

7. What are some ways in which this film affected your feelings about education and getting an education?

8. What are some lines in the film that struck you as memorable?

9. What is the floor plan of Rita's house? And of Frank's?

10. How does Rita's language change from the beginning to the end of the film?

11. How does music contribute to the film?

Reflections and Student Responses

For the discussion, I asked each student which question(s) she had chosen to concentrate on and how she answered it (them). The resulting discussion was richer than I could ever have imagined, with each student contributing observations in her own areas of strength and, consequently, expanding all of our understandings of the film. Students were clearly able to appreciate different intelligences at work, commenting, "I didn't notice that," or "How do you remember all that?" or "I never would have drawn that connection," or "I never thought of that," and other similar remarks. I could not have asked for a better demonstration of multiple intelligences!

Field Trip Lesson

Materials   List of questions related to the field trip; *Lyddie,* by Katherine Paterson, New York, Puffin Books, 1994

To extend our study of women's history and to prepare for our reading of the novel *Lyddie,* our class visited the restored textile mills in Lowell, Massachusetts. Students had already completed some nonfiction readings about the history of the mills. I developed the following set of questions, each intended to address a specific intelligence, about the trip. Again, I handed the questions out in advance and asked students to pick one or two to keep in mind during their visit.

1. Make a list of the most expressive words you can think of that would describe the information, experiences, and sensations you had during the visit.

2. What repeated activities—for example, hearing bells, climbing stairs, operating machinery—did you notice in the mill girls' lives? How many times would they repeat them during the course of a day, a week, a month, a year?

3. What things did you notice most about the appearance of the mill? The boardinghouse?

4. How do you think the mill girls' relationships with each other were affected by their work?

5. How might a mill girl's experience be represented in a timeline or flow chart?

6. What kind of natural objects might a mill girl collect to remind her of the outdoors while she worked?

7. How might a mill girl's experience be represented in a work of art?

8. What sounds did you notice most in the mill?

9. Try to repeat the motions you had to make while operating your machine or doing another job in the mill.

10. What emotions did your experiences on the visit produce in you?

11. What parts of your body would feel the worst after a day in the mill? What could you do to make them feel better?

12. How would working in the mills affect a girl's relationships with her family at home?

13. What do you imagine the mill girls thought about while they operated their machines?

14. What would a mill girl miss the most about her outdoor life on the farm?

15. What memorable things did students, guides, or narrators say during the visit?

16. For a movie about a mill girl, what music would you use in the background for different activities and locations?

Reflections and Student Responses

The mill museum is a very hands-on experience; visitors can experience carding cotton, hand weaving, hearing and watching the power looms and, in our case, participating in a production-line simulation that led to union organizing. Because of both their prior reading and the questions, students were able to focus intensely and imaginatively on their experience, placing themselves inside it, and connecting to the past in an extremely powerful way. I believe that this connection, of which they spoke at the time, encouraged them to extend the experience further. For instance, several students refused to take the elevator and instead ran down four flights of spiral stairs as the mill girls had to do in order to know what that felt like. Their discussions and writings following the trip were direct and personal, and their reading of *Lyddie* was enormously enhanced by this focused experience.

Discussion seems to work best when it goes around the class person by person. Students often feel that their contributions are of little value, particularly when they are unfamiliar with nontraditional approaches, and may not be willing to volunteer their observations. Expecting everyone to have an observation and valuing each helps to bolster confidence.

Extensions

If you want to encourage students to use unfamiliar intelligences, you might cut the questions into separate slips and have students select them at random. Alternatively, you might simply assign students questions.

To encourage students to think about the theory of multiple intelligences, you might assign them the task of coming up with similar MI-based questions for an activity.

— Problem du Jour —

Bonnie Fortini

Bonnie found this type of MI-inspired assignment particularly effective in a multilevel class.

Subject   Math

Time   This can vary from a few minutes to a few hours or more, depending on the complexity of the problem. Because my class is run in a lab setting, the students are free to work on the problem at any time.

Materials   Manipulative materials and props appropriate for the given problem; pens, pencils, markers; paper for computation and final presentation; work sheet listing the Problem du Jour

Background

My math class is multilevel with ABE and GED/High School Diploma students. The class is run as a lab where many students study independently. We are located in rural Maine where people are familiar with farm animals.

The Lesson

These minilessons provide opportunities for students to solve problems using manipulatives. I find that leaving the questions a little ambiguous and open to interpretation prompts communication among students and fosters mathematical thinking.

In my introduction to this activity, I emphasize two things to the students: This work is intended to give them some entertaining practice in mastering a particular math skill, and there is no one correct answer to the problem presented.

I set out the appropriate materials, including the Problem du Jour. All students are encouraged to try the problem on their own or with other students. I do not become involved any further in the students' work unless they request it. If students have a lot of difficulty, I try to ask questions that I think will help them solve the problem.

The following sample Problem du Jour helped students practice the procedures involved in converting fractions, decimals, and percents. I placed eight small, plastic animals onto a sheet of paper on which I had written several prompt questions:

1.   What fraction describes the part of this group that may be classified as farm animals?

2.   Write the decimal version of the fraction from your answer above.

3.   What would be the proper form for that answer if it were expressed as a percentage?

If students found this exercise too easy, I asked them to write some more difficult problems for others to solve, letting them use these or other materials.

Reflections and Student Responses

In planning this activity, I hoped to engage the following intelligences in these ways:

o   Logical-mathematical, through the content

o   Interpersonal, by allowing group and pair work

o   Spatial, by using objects, arrangements, and patterns, including the phrasing of the questions and tasks to be done

o   Linguistic, through the demonstration and presentation of student work

o   Naturalistic, through sorting and categorizing

These types of exercises made math seem more engaging to students. There were a number of reasons why this format worked in my math lab, including the sense of fun and teamwork it engendered.

MI-inspired Language Arts and ESOL Lessons

— Gimme Five: Your Hand as a Writing Guide —

Lezlie Rocka

Lezlie Rocka combined her understanding of multisensory education and MI theory to produce these lessons.

> I found Lezlie's hand activity excellent for students just beginning to write an essay. I showed them how to use the hand to write their main idea and the three middle fingers to write the supporting reasons. This really helped keep the introductory paragraph succinct and to the point. Without doing it this way, students tend to start right in with their example in the intro. Now when students are writing an essay, the first thing they do after brainstorming is draw their hand on their paper. I've had nothing but positive comments about this method.
>
> ~ Helen Sablan, AMI Sourcebook Pilot Teacher, 1999

Subject   Language arts

Curriculum Objective

To construct sentences, paragraphs, and essays

Time   Depends on the skill level of students. It took my students about 2 months working 1 $^1\!/_2$ hours per week to learn this technique.

Materials   Pens or pencils, paper, poster board, colored pencils and markers

Background

My beginning ABE students read at a third- to fifth-grade level. Many of them have learning difficulties or are learning English as nonnative speakers.

The Unit

Below I describe the systematic way I teach my students to construct sentences, paragraphs, and essays. This approach works well with students who have little confidence in their writing ability.

Lesson 1: Sentences

I began this lesson by reminding my students that they already know how to write stories. If I asked them to tell me about their children or themselves, they could do that. I told them that I was now going to show them how to write a report or an essay.

I posted this question on the board: "Do you think we should take military action against Iraq?" We then discussed how one might answer this question in writing. Often students simply answered "yes" or "no." I told them that they were halfway there, but that they needed to be clearer about which question they were answering.

I showed them that there is an easy way to answer in writing any question that they are asked. I held my thumb up in an "everything is A-OK!" position and said, "Think of your thumb as the answer to a question. This answer could also be called the main idea of your writing. To answer any question in writing, you need a complete sentence. You can even use the words from the question in your sentence."[*]

---

[*] The idea of the paragraph hand was introduced to me at an Adult Education Institute sponsored by SABES, Southeast and New Bedford Public Schools Division of Adult and Continuing Education, on March 16, 1996. The workshop was called *Paragraph and Essay Structure for the Visual Learner.* Presented by Pam Drouin, Teacher, Bristol Community College, Fall River, MA, and Andrea Petrucelli, Norfolk County House of Correction, LD Team Member.

We practiced answering the question in a complete sentence. "No, I do not think we should take military action against Iraq" or "Yes, I do think we should…." I explained to them that this format helps the reader know which question they are answering.

We continued practicing and exploring main idea sentences with these activities:

o   Sensory Learning: We outlined our right hand and shaded the thumb a particular color. We then underlined our main idea sentence with this same color.

o   Blind Practices: I had some students who were having difficulty seeing or hearing the question say or guess what the topic was on the basis of the answers written by their classmates.

o   Practice: I kept asking and having students ask questions until giving complete answers came naturally to them.

An example question and (edited) student response follows.

Q: People come to school for different reasons. Why are you here?

A: I know that I can learn if I don't give up.

Lesson 2: Paragraphs

I began the second lesson by reminding my students that to begin to write a paragraph, all they need to do is look at their thumbs. I reviewed this by asking, "What does your thumb stand for?" The students responded by saying, "An answer or a main idea in a complete sentence."

Again, I put a question on the board and asked the students to write an answer. I reinforced the idea that this "thumb" would become the main idea of their paragraphs.

I continued by telling the students that they needed to inform the reader why they thought the way they did or why they gave their particular answer. I told them that they do this by giving three reasons and that these ideas are also known as details or supporting sentences. I also told the students that these three sentences could be represented by the index, middle, and ring fingers. These three "fingers" must talk about the subject (the "thumb"). They also need to be complete sentences like the "thumb" sentence.

Once the students had written these sentences, we looked in books to see how other authors had organized their paragraphs. The students noticed that paragraphs are indented, that new sentences follow the previous period, and that sentences have periods and capitals.

For many of my students, learning how to use all this information was new. Each time they wrote a paragraph, they used their hand to check to see if they had everything necessary. We continued practicing and exploring paragraphs.

o   Sensory Learning: Using our outlined hand from above, we now shaded in the three fingers with a color different from that of the thumb. We then underlined the lines in our paragraphs that coincided with the representative colors on our drawn hands. If the students asked about the pinky, I told them that we would talk about it later when we began writing essays.

o   Oral Paragraphs: We told a story about each person in the room. For example, "Rita looks pretty today. She has a nice hair-do. She has on a nice-looking outfit. She also has a big smile on her face." I pointed out that these stories were just like paragraphs.

o   Paragraph Puzzles: The students cut up their paragraphs into separate sentences and the other students tried to piece them together in the correct order.

o   More Paragraph Puzzles: I wrote two paragraphs on one subject, giving a pro and a con view. Students unscrambled my paragraphs, and we debated which paragraph was the best or most correct one. We discussed that, as long as you can validate a main idea with three supporting sentences (or three "fingers"), any opinion is reasonable.

    o   Paragraph Playhouse Theater: My class performed as the Paragraph Puzzle Players for a colleague's class. Our class wrote a paragraph together, edited it, and then put in purposeful mistakes. We printed the incorrect version on poster board, cut it up into sentence strips, and had different students each take one of the sentence strips to hold up in front of the other class. Students then planned how they were going to scramble themselves up so that the sentences would be out of order and figured out how they were going to give directions to the other class so that they could correct the errors.

The emcee made her own cue cards detailing what she wanted to say to the other class. She wanted them to know exactly what they had to do. Her dialogue read, "Hi, we are here to do a presentation about a paragraph puzzle. This puzzle is out of order. You'll have to guess which one is the main idea and which are the details. You guys need to put this puzzle in order. You guys need to figure out punctuation marks and correct spelling. Punctuation means capital letters."

After this project, a student, who had been having a hard time with writing paragraphs, proudly said, "I understand a paragraph."

An example of a student-edited paragraph follows.

> I know that I can learn if I don't give up. I hope to learn as much as I can. This way, I can keep helping my sons learn. I think the more I study, the more I will learn.

Lesson 3: Essays

I explained that we were going to begin writing essays. My students usually become quite intimidated when I mention this. Therefore, showing them my A-OK thumb, I reminded them that all they need to begin an essay is an opening sentence. At this point, they knew how to write a topic sentence, so they answered whatever question I put on the board. I then had them recall that they knew what to do next, because all they needed to do was write a paragraph to further the idea expressed in the topic sentence. Once again, they wrote their paragraphs.

Next, I taught the students how to expand their paragraphs into essays. I said, "To turn this paragraph into an essay, you take your 'index finger' sentence and rewrite it as a new paragraph; it has now become the 'thumb' of a new paragraph. You now need an 'index,' 'middle,' and 'ring finger' for this new paragraph. You do this by giving three details or supporting sentences about this new 'thumb.' These three 'fingers' must talk about the subject of the 'thumb' of this new paragraph. These also need to be complete sentences, just like the 'thumb' sentence."

Some students guessed what they needed to do next. They took the "middle finger" from the first paragraph. It became a "thumb" of a third paragraph, and they gave it three new "fingers."

I informed the students that they had to do this once more with the "ring finger" sentence of the first paragraph. By this time, many students seemed to know what to do.

Finally, I added the "pinky" to the essay. I taught them that this was the end or the conclusion to the essay. I put the thumb and pinky together and said, "It's time to wrap it up!"

I told the students that the conclusion could be a restatement of the very first sentence, or "thumb," of the essay. They had to repeat the whole reason for writing their essays. I showed them how they could change the wording a bit but keep the same idea, or they could write a conclusion with either a feeling for what they wrote about or a hope for the future.

    o   Sensory Learning: Using the outlined hand from above, the students now shaded the pinky a color different from that of the thumb and three fingers. They then underlined the lines in their paragraphs that coincided with the representative colors on their drawn hands.

    o   Sharing: Students read their essays aloud. (They were usually shocked at how cohesive their writing was.)

After they felt comfortable with this pattern, I told students that this method is only a basic outline to guide them and that it is ok to adjust the pattern to fit what they want to say.

An example of an edited student essay follows,

> I know that I can learn if I don't give up. I hope to learn as much as I can. This way I can keep helping my sons learn. I think the more I study, the more I will learn.
>
> I hope to learn as much as I can. I come to school every day. My teacher teaches me how to read, spell, study maps, and do math. Then whatever I learn, I try to remember.
>
> I want to keep helping my sons learn. When my boys come home from school, I try to help them. First, I help them read and understand what they have to do. Then I check their work. I am proud of both of them for sticking with it because sometimes the homework is hard.
>
> I think the more I study, the more I will learn. Sometimes it is hard to study because after I study, I can't remember what I have read. So, I have to work on remembering.
>
> I hope that someday I can remember things. I know that I can learn if I don't give up.

Reflections and Student Responses

On the basis of my understanding of MI Theory, I used projects and activities to help students develop their writing skills. I thought that having students express and process the information in as many ways as possible would assist them in using their strongest intelligences to understand the information.

I liked to use questions and topics pertaining to students' lives and the world around them. I found this a good way to spark conversation on important or interesting issues. Some students struggled with answering the question that was asked and relating the supporting sentences back to the main idea, but they improved with increased practice.

The students responded positively to teaching other students during the Paragraph Playhouse activity, even though the work involved was difficult for them. One student said that it was good for her to perform in public because it helped her speak her mind.

When teaching other students, my students wanted to be sure that they spoke in a way that the other students could understand. They were especially sensitive because the class we were to teach was at a lower skill level than our class in writing.

— Let Your Fingers Do the Walking —

Lezlie Rocka

In this lesson Lezlie shows how she extended her multisensory lesson to include MI.

Subject   Language arts
Curriculum Objective
            To develop comprehension and research skills
Time   Approximately 1¹/₂ hours per session
Materials *If You Traveled on the Underground Railroad,* by Ellen Levine, Scholastic, 1993; paper, pencils

Background

My beginning ABE students read at a third- to fifth-grade level. Many of them have learning difficulties or are learning English as nonnative speakers. All seem to have difficulty decoding, comprehending, and retaining what they have read. How to extract facts out of text is a skill they need to be taught directly.

The Lesson

The following lesson highlights a method for gathering facts from written material. I have found this technique particularly successful for beginning ABE students.

Prereading

I began by asking the students these questions:

o   Have you ever heard of the Underground Railroad?

o   Do you know anything about it?

o   Do you have any guesses about what it might be?

I reminded the students that they already know how to read a story and follow what the author is writing about. I told them that I was going to show them how to pull facts out of what they had read and write this information down in an outline form.

I asked the students to remember what they needed to think about when they were writing a paragraph. They recalled that they could use their hands to guide their writing. (See the lesson Gimme Five: Your Hand as a Writing Guide.) I told them that they could use a similar method to help them pull facts out of what they had read.

I directed their attention to the book *If You Traveled on the Underground Railroad.* First, I asked them to tell me what they thought the book was about. I clued them into the fact that the main idea of the whole book could often be found in the title. I showed them how to write this information at the margin on the top of their papers and told them that this would be the title of their notes: The Underground Railroad.

The Main Idea, or "Thumb"

I told the students that they could usually figure out the main idea of a particular section of a book by looking at the page or chapter titles. I pointed out this information to them and asked them what they thought they were going to read about first. The students realized that they were going to find out how the Underground Railroad got its name. I showed them how to add this information to their notes:

The Underground Railroad

    How the Underground Railroad got its name

The Facts or "Fingers"

I continued by telling the students that they now were going to find information to support the main idea by reading the book. I suggested that they might be able to find more than three facts and that this was fine. I told them that they had to decide which facts were the most important and write them under the main idea.

Reading

The students read pages 5 through 6, stopping at the end of every paragraph and discussing which facts they would like to write in their notes. They took turns reading aloud. They used their fingers, pencils, or bookmarks to help guide their eyes. As they read, I coached them on how to use various decoding strategies, such as focusing on the beginning and ending sounds of any words with which they were unfamiliar. We discussed the meanings of any difficult words and reread the passages whenever necessary. We also included facts that we could glean from the pictures in the book. When they had finished, the students had collected the following information for their notes.

The Underground Railroad

How the Underground Railroad got its name

1. Tice Davids escaped.
2. His owner couldn't find him.
3. His owner said, "He must have gone on an underground road."
4. The name stuck.
5. It was named "Underground" because it was secret.
6. It was named "Railroad" because it seemed to run regularly.

Postreading

After the students had gathered facts about the Underground Railroad, they worked on the following assignment.

Materials Notes from their reading; writing and drawing paper; Play-Doh®

Directions

Using only your notes, work alone, or with a partner or group, and choose one of the following projects:

1. Put a fact from your notes into a rhythm.
2. Draw a picture or use Play-Doh® to show one of your facts.
3. Act out one of your facts.
4. Discuss or write how you would feel if it were you experiencing one of your facts.
5. Write or discuss all the things you think someone would have to think about if he were escaping.

For a detailed multisensory method of dissecting any text, I suggest that you read *Report Form Comprehension Guide,* by Victoria E. Greene and Mary Lee Enfield, Ph.D. (Language Circle® Enterprises, PO Box 20631, Bloomington, MN 55420, http://www.projectread.com).

Reflections and Student Responses

By concentrating on the pictures to gather information and by selecting from the project choices in the postreading portion of the lesson, the students had options as to how they could process and express the information found in the chapter. These different options allowed the students to "encode," or take in information, in many ways. This made it easier for the students to draw upon their various intelligences to help them glean as much information from the text as possible.

Extensions

The students could use their notes to do any of the following projects:
- o   Perform a play based on the story.
- o   Create a class album using the student notes, project work, and photographs of the students taken as they work on their activities.
- o   Illustrate the story using story strips, like a cartoon strip.

— Parts-of-Speech Trading Game —

Wendy Quiñones

Wendy designed this game as a way to review English grammar. It encourages students to draw upon many of their strongest intelligences as they follow the directions for the play.

Subject   Language arts
Curriculum Objective
               To learn parts of speech
Time   15 to 20 minutes for each round
Materials   A set of "trading cards" (I make them on laser-printer business card forms, but index cards or slips of paper work just as well). These are in matched pairs, one card containing a word and the other its correct part of speech (verb, adjective, noun, and so on). For example, I put *cat* on one card and *noun* on the other. For each round, the game requires four pairs of cards for each player, with one pair for each part of speech you want to include in the mix. The words must always be in pairs, with a correct part-of-speech label for each word used. Envelopes for storing the trading cards—one for all the nouns, one for the verbs, and so on.
               A game sheet for each player.

Background

Many of my students are eager to learn parts of speech in order to improve their writing. After having tried various methods with mixed success, I wanted to find an engaging way that students could teach and reinforce each other, taking advantage of their high interpersonal intelligences. This trading game was the result.

The Lesson

I began this lesson by assembling sets of four word/label pairs for each player, each pair representing a different part of speech. I mixed the cards thoroughly. Each player drew eight cards at random from the pile. The players then began trying to correctly match their pairs, trading cards with each other when they had mismatches among the cards they had drawn. The game ended when all players had four correct pairs. If there were any mismatches at the end, the players had to work cooperatively to rethink the way they had matched words and labels and reorganize them until all pairs of words and labels matched. When at last the players had agreed on the overall solution, they wrote their words on their game sheet and handed their papers in to me.

For ease in organization, I kept the cards separated into envelopes by parts of speech—one for nouns, another for verbs, and so forth. Then whenever I wanted to use the game, all that was necessary was to pull out the required number of pairs of whichever parts of speech were to be used. This organization also made it easy for students to put the cards away so I did not have to do it all the time!

Reflections and Student Responses

The first time I used this game, I had students working with only four parts of speech: nouns, adjectives, verbs, and adverbs. It worked wonderfully—students were moving around, asking each other questions (e.g., "What does an adjective do again?" "But if somebody's hopeful, isn't that an action?"). The next time I tried all eight parts of speech and it was simply too much! Clearly, the instruction I had given beforehand was not sufficient to counteract all the possibilities for confusion. Therefore, until your students are comfortable with them, it is probably better to use fewer parts of speech. The game can be individualized for the specific parts that are giving your students trouble, and you can throw in as many trick words as you want—words that can be both nouns and verbs, for example. Because they can produce such confusion in trying to match the pairs and such lively discussion about how to resolve the difficulties, these "tricks" are a terrific way of demonstrating that words can have multiple uses.

Extensions

One of my colleagues used it very successfully with math problems in a GED/Adult Diploma program (See Math Review Card Game). I can also see using it for vocabulary with either English or ESOL students, historical dates or figures, or whatever your imagination can come up with. The important thing here is that students are teaching each other and using their interpersonal intelligence to process the learning.

— Activities to Inspire Reading for Meaning —

Lezlie Rocka

Lezlie learned that MI-inspired activities helped her students better comprehend what they had read, and this, in turn, led to increased retention of information.

Subject   Reading
Curriculum Objective
            To develop reading comprehension
Time   Approximately $1^1/_2$ hours per session
Materials Books for everyone, pencils, paper, colored pencils, drawing paper, Play-Doh®, magazines, scissors, glue, plus any other materials your students might need depending on the projects they decide to do.

Background

My beginning ABE students read at a third- to fifth-grade level. Many of them have learning difficulties or are learning English as nonnative speakers. All seem to have difficulty decoding, comprehending, and retaining what they read.

The Lesson

As a class, we read *Meet Addy*, by Connie Porter. This book, classified as historical fiction, illustrates some of the experiences slaves had while trying to escape on the Underground Railroad. Addy, the main character, is a young teen born into slavery who escapes with her mother to freedom.

The following is a sample lesson that shows how I used my understanding of MI theory to guide the students as they read Chapter 3 in this book.

Prereading

I began the group reading lesson with a prereading question based on what we were about to read. For this chapter, I asked students if they had ever had to make a really difficult decision. We then discussed or wrote about their responses.

Reading

We started reading the chapter. While reading, I coached the students in how to apply all the multisensory skills they had already learned to decode and comprehend what they were reading. I reminded the students to use their fingers, pencils, or bookmarks to help guide their eyes. I made sure to allow students ample time to apply their decoding strategies before giving a prompt. I coached the students on beginning or ending sounds of words when they needed it. We discussed difficult words and what we had read after every paragraph, rereading the paragraphs whenever necessary.

Postreading Project

We then did a postreading project. I gave the students a list of MI-informed project options from which they were to select one. One of the choices gave them the option to make up their own activity. These projects allowed students to choose how they wanted to express what they had understood about the reading.

Activities for Chapter 3 of *Meet Addy*

Directions: Working alone, with a partner, or with a group, choose one of the following projects:
1.   Draw a picture of a scene described in the chapter we read.
2.   Pick a song that you think Addy might have sung. Then either sing it or write the words.

3. Use Play-Doh® to show what you think the plantation where Addy and her family live looks like.

4. Write a letter from Addy to her Poppa.

5. Figure out how many worms could actually fit into someone's mouth. (In the book, the plantation foreman, as a punishment, forces Addy to eat all the worms she missed while deworming the tobacco leaves.)

6. Pretend you are Addy in one of the scenes and act it out.

7. Make a list of the events you remember in this chapter. Put these events in the order in which they occurred.

8. Make up your own project for this chapter.

Discuss what you did with the class.

Reflections and Student Responses

With the postreading portion of this lesson, students had a choice in how they could show what they had gleaned from the reading. I tried to include choices that would allow students to process the readings using different intelligences. This is what one of my students had to say about that,

> We've been reading about cultures and slavery. Generations really, times that I've never known before ... that I'm learning now. You never think about it 'til you start reading about these true stories about people's lives, it's horrible. So, you kind of get emotional when you're reading some of it. That's why I like to do the role plays. I always like to do the role play because I want to feel it a little bit. And I listen very carefully to it to see if I got it.

She also said this about role playing: "At the same time we're learning, we're having a good time with it."

I found that many students liked making lists of what they remembered from the chapter. One very quiet student was the first to suggest that she could make a list, even though it had not been offered in the original selection of choices for the postreading activities. She simply said, "I could write down what I remember." After she mentioned this activity, we decided to add it to the list of choices.

While doing the projects, students often explained different aspects of the text to each other whenever the need arose. At one point, one student was coaching another through a scene in which she was playing Addy. The student could not remember her next lines. Instead of telling her the exact words to say, the coach set the scene for her, so that she could come up with her own words.

It is important to discuss the projects afterwards. I was surprised at what the students had understood from their reading. They too were surprised at themselves and their recollections. My students are usually like sieves when they read; the information flows through the holes. However, when they do projects about what they have read, this seems to plug up the holes, and they remember more.

These projects take up much of the reading time. At first, this was difficult for me, but I kept coming back to this thought: If they are not remembering what they have read, there is not much point in reading. I saw that retention seemed to improve when students began using different ways to express what they understood and remembered from the reading. Students expressed what they understood about writing or reading through their projects and activities. I assumed that students would choose projects that corresponded most closely with their strongest intelligences and would be more likely to comprehend and remember the material. I observed a positive cycle of comprehension and retention.

For example, the students expressed what they had understood in the reading in the form of a skit. By acting out the scene, the students then understood better what was happening when they went back to their reading. This helped them remember the next chapter they read. It also seemed to help them understand what came next in the book.

Extensions

I have listed below some other activities that students could also do as postreading projects. Your imagination and that of your students is the limit. You can be as broad or specific as you like.

Word Smart (Linguistic Intelligence)
o   Memorize and recite dialogue or a character's speech.
o   Write a poem about a character or the chapter.

Logic Smart [Math Smart] (Logical-Mathematical Intelligence)
o   List the events that occurred in this chapter; put these events in order.
o   Make a timeline of the events in this chapter.

Picture Smart (Spatial Intelligence)
o   Make a story map of what happened in the chapter.
o   Make a collage of the chapter.
o   Make a cartoon strip of the chapter.

Body Smart (Bodily-Kinesthetic Intelligence)
o   Walk across the room the way you think Addy would have walked in this scene.
o   Read Addy's dialogue and make the face she would have worn while speaking.

Music Smart (Musical Intelligence)
o   Make up a song (rap, country, and so on).
o   Choose background music for a specific scene as though it were a movie.
o   Make up a rhythm to express the feeling in a scene from this chapter.

People Smart (Interpersonal Intelligence)
o   With a partner or a group discuss how you think Addy felt in a specific scene.
o   Discuss the difference in lifestyle between the slaves and the slave owners in this chapter.

Self Smart (Intrapersonal Intelligence)
o   Discuss how you might have felt in the same situation as one of the book's characters.

Nature Smart (Naturalist Intelligence)
o   Make a list of the things you learned about growing tobacco from this story.
o   Discuss what the land looked like where Addy grew up.

Upon finishing the book, the class might work on one of these projects:
o   Make a scrapbook detailing Addy's life.
o   Perform a play based on the story.
o   Sew an outfit like the one Addy might have worn.
o   Cook and eat a meal that Addy and her family might have eaten.
o   Create a class album of the story, using all the work the students have done on their projects and photographs of them engaged in these tasks.

— Using Personally Relevant Literature —

Carol Beima

Carol built on Lezlie's Activities to Inspire Reading for Meaning lesson.

Subject   Language arts
Curriculum Objective
              To develop reading comprehension
Time   50-minute class sessions, 4 days per week
Materials   Copies for each student of *Baby,* a short novel by Patricia MacLachlan; assorted art supplies including colored pencils, markers, and drawing paper; assorted resource books, including dictionaries, encyclopedias, and poetry collections; a cassette or CD player, or computers with Internet access capable of playing selected music samples

Background

The class that read *Baby* typically consisted of 12 to 15 ABE students whose reading levels ranged from third- to sixth-grade levels. The majority were women in their 30s and 40s, many of them mothers. About half were ESOL students, whereas some others had learning difficulties in reading.

The Lesson

Before we began to read the novel *Baby,* I talked to the class about multiple intelligences and had the students complete the AMI Survey to prepare them to try some MI-based activities that would be different from ordinary reading comprehension questions.

To begin the novel, I led the group in some prereading activities, such as predicting what the book is about from the title. Then I read Chapter 1 aloud to the students, pausing to ask comprehension questions, make comments, and listen to student responses. The students read along from their own copies. The next session, the students reread the chapter individually or in small groups. I then gave them a sheet of choice activities related to Chapter 1 that I hoped would engage a variety of intelligences.

As we continued reading the book, we began each session with sharing any projects and ideas, and then moved on to read new chapters. Sometimes students chose to read aloud, and other times they preferred to listen and read along as I read. I prepared discussion questions and a vocabulary list ahead of time. I wanted to ask questions and make suggestions for further learning that could appeal to different intelligences. For example, in Chapter 14, there is a scene where characters are looking at clouds. I thought some further study might appeal to the students who had indicated a high naturalist intelligence. I suggested that they might find information about some different cloud types and shapes. Some looked up pictures in an encyclopedia and shared their discoveries later. We also compared the descriptions of the East Coast winter clouds to what we observe in the Pacific Northwest.

Choice Activities for Chapters 3 and 4 of *Baby*

Work on one or more of these projects either alone or with other classmates.

o   Make a list of some of the figurative language used in these chapters.

o   Share a hand game you know that people teach to babies. Tell which country it comes from.

o   Mama insists that Papa call the baby by her name, Sophie. Write about the history of your name or draw the letters in a way that especially fits you.

o   Sing a lullaby you know, read lullabies from other countries, or write a new one.

o   Draw a favorite scene from these chapters using pencils, markers, or paints.

o   Begin a journal and write a few sentences about the emotions you feel after reading each chapter.

o   With some classmates, act out a scene we read in these chapters.

o   Reread the chapters and write or discuss how you understand the actions of the different family members now that you know about the death of their baby.

o   Make a list of reasons a young woman might not be able to care for her child. Then make a second list of actions she might take.

o   Write a letter asking someone to care for your child while you are unable to do so.

Reflections and Student Responses

The students enjoyed the initial activities for *Baby*. Many of the characters were unique and several students chose to draw them, laughing and talking as they brought some of the details to life in pictures, such as Papa drinking whiskey and tap dancing on the table. The students enjoyed listening to and singing along with many of the songs referred to in the book. I especially liked the discussion and song sharing that occurred when students reflected on lullabies they knew from their own childhood and cultures. The importance of one's name was significant in the novel, and another favorite sharing time was when the students discussed how and why they came to have a particular name.

In the opening chapter, the family shared unbaked cake batter. A deaf student's interpreter got into the MI spirit and brought in the ingredients for spice cake, just as they had done in the story. The student then prepared the batter and served it in cups for everyone to try. This activity helped him interact more with the hearing students in the class. This student is a talented artist, so some of the MI choices drew others to him as he shared through the visual-spatial projects.

The MI projects seemed to inspire more laughter than I usually observe as well as deeper personal sharing and involvement with others in the class. Often, when a student did a choice activity on her own, there was some eager sharing with other classmates and me before we got to the reading.

The choice projects were particularly valuable in introducing the novel and getting students engaged at the beginning. However, doing choice projects after every chapter required too much teacher preparation and took time away from reading. Having time to read some new material each day was important for the students to feel they were progressing. Consequently, I made the daily sharing of choice projects optional. It gave individual students the opportunity to do more as they chose and to model possibilities for others in a nonthreatening way.

Overall, I found that MI-based activities were a good way to introduce a concept, book, or other learning activity. I found that more students worked on projects outside of class and brought in more resources when I encouraged them in these varied ways informed by my MI lens. The students really liked the variety of the choice activities, and that prompted improved attendance and participation in reading both in and outside of class.

— Waxing Poetic —

Judy Hickey

AMI Sourcebook Pilot Teacher Judy Hickey developed these lessons in the course of her exploration of MI theory, inspired by the lessons developed by the AMI teacher–researchers.

Subject   Language arts
Curriculum Objective
                Develop a working knowledge of literary terms to analyze literature
Time   Set up in the second half of an 80-minute class. Projects are due a week later.
Materials   We have an "Art Cart," a movable feast on a library cart full of scissors, glue, markers, colored paper, magazines, and so forth; glossary of terms

Background

This is a pre-GED class called Literature and the Arts, taught to adults at a fifth- to seventh-grade reading level. The class had been given a list of literary terms and their definitions (see Interpreting Literature and Poetry Glossary following Lesson 2) at the beginning of a 7-week cycle. We spent 3 weeks analyzing drama excerpts using these terms. Then we focused on other fiction, such as short stories or poetry, and used these same terms. The following MI activity was a way of having students study the terms and learn them for a final test that required matching the term with its definition as well as analyzing a piece of text they had never seen before.

Lesson 1: Analyzing Literature

To set the context, I talked briefly about how we all have different strengths. Then I gave out the assignment options that follow.

I talked students through each option, encouraging them to choose whatever project appealed to them. I showed them a montage I had done using the literary term "mood." I asked them which of the three plays we had read they thought the montage represented, and they got it right. I demonstrated an example of each project, if they asked about it. I did a pantomime of the four kinds of "conflict," asking them which kind of conflict it represented; they got it easily. I showed them what a timeline or flow chart looked like. By the time we went through the choices, I was hearing the now familiar sounds of "Oooo! I'm going to do that one," or, "Sebrita, would you do a skit with me?"

Analyzing Literature: Choose One

Word Smart

Write a 150-word paper using the literary term you have chosen. Write about one of the "characters," and their qualities. Describe the "conflict." How does it get resolved? Discuss the "theme." Support it with lines from the play. Use stage directions to describe the "setting" you have in mind.

Math Smart

Make a timeline or flow chart of the major events in the play. Follow the ups and downs that the major protagonist must undergo.

Body Smart

Develop and perform a skit or a small drama that demonstrates your chosen literary term. If you are using "conflict," act out each kind and have the class guess which kind it is. You may also come dressed as your literary term, and dance out the "theme."

Music Smart

Write a song or rap about your literary term. Put the definition or an example of "mood," "symbol," "imagery," or whatever your term is, to a familiar tune.

Picture Smart

Draw a picture of your literary term in action in one of the play excerpts we read. Alternatively, put a montage of pictures that illustrates your term together. If there are good "similes" or "metaphors," you could illustrate the two unlike things being compared. If there is a "personification," show a picture of the nonliving thing and another picture showing the human quality demonstrated.

People Smart

Set up a talk show or an interview between you and the literary term of your choice. Perhaps you could ask "conflict" what he or she adds to any good work of fiction, or ask "mood" how she manages to move people.

Self Smart

Is this play telling a truth about life? What is the philosophy of life being "played out" through the story and the characters? How is it connected to "theme"? (Although this is introspective, it still takes some Word Smarts to either tell the class or write it out and then read it.)

Reflections and Student Responses

There were several highlights from my students' presentations.

o One woman brought in a garbage bag full of materials to create her setting for Beth Henley's "Crimes of the Heart." She laid out a tablecloth, matching party plates, some cake, a small vase of flowers, and balloons. She then wrote a poem on a birthday card to the character being celebrated. The class then had to guess what her literary term was and which "smart" she was using. They realized how much the literary terms overlap. Some guessed "setting," and others thought "mood." Because she had written and read a poem, they also said she included "word smart." This occasioned a good discussion of how all of these elements are present in good fiction. Her term was "setting," but she also created the "mood" of pathos through the poem, which required "word smart." She had also used her "body smart" to imagine and arrange the setting with such authenticity.

o Another stunning presentation was from a hearing- and sight-impaired woman who had said barely a word in class. She got up and acted out each of the kinds of conflict (person vs. person, community, nature, or self). (At the end, she got a standing ovation from the class.) She wore all black to suggest the darkness of all kinds of struggles.

o There were at least two montages, two timelines, and a drawing.

The students did well on the final test. They matched the definitions to the terms and then had to analyze a bit of literature they had never seen before. I am sure practicing the literary terms using literature, as well as through the "smarts," contributed to their overall success.

Lesson 2: Poetry Presentations

o Choose a poem that you like personally. It should be no more or less than 20 lines. (It can be one that you write yourself.)

o Read it to the class.

o Prepare a paraphrase (a rewording) of your poem.

o Prepare one of the following presentations to help the class experience the power of the poem for you.

Word Smart

Write a 150-word paper explaining why the poem is important to you.

Math Smart

Make a timeline or flow chart on large paper and walk the class through the important events or turning points in the poem.

Body Smart

Act out your poem by turning it into a drama or use material you have at home to create a sculpture that tells the class something about your poem.

Picture Smart

Draw your poem or represent it in a montage of pictures.

Music Smart

Write a song using the main ideas of your poem or put some of the ideas of the poem to a familiar tune. You could also put your poem into rap form.

People Smart

Describe how you experience the ideas of this poem in your own life, and why you think it will be important for others to understand your poem.

Self Smart

Describe how this poem expresses many of the same feelings you have about life. How does the poem give you courage to live your own life?

Reflections and Student Responses

The response from my students was great. They especially enjoyed being able to choose poetry they really liked. One woman sang her poem and danced to it. Two of the students shared poems by Tupac Shakur and talked about the impact he had on their lives. Two students wrote original poems. There were artistic representations and skits. One man presented Bryant's "We Wear the Mask" and held a wonderful homemade smiling mask up to his face whenever he referred to the metaphorical mask. One woman shared a montage of her son's pictures; he had been shot the previous year while sitting on her front steps. Her poem of choice was "We Remember Them" from the *Judaism Prayer Book*.

As usual, I had everyone reflect on which smart was the smart of choice after each presentation. The students could easily see that there were overlaps. They noticed that the word *smart* dominated in that it took words to express the people, self, and even the body smart skits.

Interpreting Literature and Poetry Glossary

Plot or Narrative: A series of actions that make up a work of fiction. The story line.

Conflict: Every story has complications that make the action move or rise. The four types of conflict include:

- o Person vs. person (Child and parent or friend and friend.)

- o Person vs. community (Rosa Parks sat down in the bus and sparked the civil rights movement.)

- o Person vs. himself or herself (Staying clean sometimes demands a moment by moment decision.)

- o Person vs. some natural or unnatural force in life (The storm battered them until they ran inside.)

Climax: Within the plot there will be a high point or a turning point that is the climax.

Characters: Are presented through their speech, actions, descriptions, and through what others say about them.

Point of View: The person through whose eyes the story is told, the voice through which the writer tells the story.

- o First-person point of view: The story or poem is seen through the speaker, the "I."

- o Third-person point of view: The story or poem is seen from the outside and refers to the characters as "he" or "she."

- o Omniscient point of view: This view can see into the heart and mind of the character.

Setting: The time and place of the story, book, or poem.

Theme: The central idea or main message of the story, book, or poem.

Tone: The author's style that suggests his or her attitude toward the subject.

Mood: The atmosphere or emotional effect created by the author.

Figurative Language: Words that appeal to the reader's emotions and imagination.

Image/Imagery: Figurative language that appeals to the senses: see, hear, taste, smell, touch, feel, think. (The red and green candy cane smelled strongly of peppermint.)

Simile: Figurative language in which two unlike things are compared using like or as. (She was *as* lovely *as* a rose. She blew in *like* the wind.)

Metaphor: Figurative language in which two unlike things are compared without the use of like or as. (She was a rose. All the world is a stage.)

Symbol: Object or language that represents an idea. (The cross represents Christianity.)

Onomatopoeia: The use of words whose sounds imitate their meanings. Sound-imitating words include buzz, screech, boom, crash. (The owl's sorrowful *hoot* could be heard in the dark forest. The wild *whoosh* of the water swept away everything in its path.)

Rhythm, Rhyme, Meter: The rise and fall of stressed words and syllables (When I was *one* and *twenty*, I *heard* a *wise* man *say*, "give *crowns* and *pounds* and *pennies*, but *not* your *heart* away.")

Alliteration: The repetition of beginning consonant sounds. (The Wildness of the Wind Worried her. Susie Sells Seashells down by the Seashore.)

Personification: Something nonhuman comes alive when presented as having human qualities. (The winds *moaned*. The moon *smiled*.)

— Choose 3: Paint Your Way Into Writing —

Martha Jean

This lesson is an example of the Choose 3 format Martha developed. For a fuller description of Martha's class and the Choose 3 approach, please see Martha's write-up under MI Lesson Formats earlier in this chapter.

> We did this activity as a prelude to writing an essay.... As soon as they read the directions, they started the drawing/painting. I was amazed at the intensity of their work. They shared the materials and commented positively on each other's work. The results were hung on the wall to brighten up the classroom.... This went much better than I had expected. I was impressed by their willingness to have their work displayed on the walls for other classes to see.
> ~ Helen Sablan, AMI Sourcebook Pilot Teacher

Subject   Language arts
Curriculum Objective
        To ease students into a writing assignment
Materials   Paint, paper, collection of pictures of paintings done by various artists

Background

I teach GED. I wanted to find a way to expand the number of learning activities that my students could experience while still preparing for the five GED exams. I was especially concerned with helping those students who experience learning difficulties.

The Lesson

This is a prewriting activity. I asked the students to think about how creating a painting is like writing an essay. I then had them select three choices to do from this list of activities:

1. Paint a picture depicting a strong feeling. Paint another showing a weak feeling.
2. Look at a piece of artwork and paint your own version.
3. Paint a shape or shapes you like.
4. Paint a repeated pattern of a shape or shapes you like.
5. Show how you can combine colors to make new colors.
6. Show, through painting, a way that your body moves.
7. Paint three numbers you like in the color(s) you think fit them.
8. Paint the rhythm of a song you know.
9. Paint how it makes you feel when you are painting.
10. With a partner, paint a design, picture, or feeling.
11. Paint three interesting words with the colors and movements that you think would match each word.

After all students who want to share their paintings have told about their choices, ask them to choose a picture of a painting that they like from the collection of prints that you have brought to class. Ask them to think about why they feel this is a great painting. How are painting and writing similar? How are they different?

Reflections and Student Responses

As I had hoped, these activities led to an interesting discussion on writing. I noted especially that my ADD students really got into this work. Something clicked for them, and their level of involvement in this lesson showed me how much they enjoyed this type of work.

— Learning English Through Movement: Making Sentences —

Terri Coustan

Terri adapted the two activities that follow from ideas she received from Kristin D. Sherman of Central Piedmont College in Charlotte, North Carolina. This easy game is one in which students can experience the word order of sentences through movement.

My grammar class is the last period and often the students seem tired. This assignment forced them to get up and move around. It also put more excitement in the lesson. At first, the students were a little hesitant, but they quickly got into the mood of the activity. The game seemed to keep their attention because it made them move around, but also because it forced them to put their book knowledge into practice. The students were laughing and seemed to be enjoying themselves. I asked them afterwards whether or not they felt it helped them, and they said that it did.

~ Lynn Pinder, AMI Sourcebook Pilot teacher

Subject   Language arts
Curriculum Objective
          Sentence formation
Time   15 minutes
Materials   9- by 12-inch pieces of cardboard and markers

Background

I teach in a family literacy program in which 17 parents come to school with their 12 preschool-aged children. The students are between the ages of 30 and 50. Most of the students in the class are Hmong from the hills of Laos. Some are struggling to communicate orally in English, whereas others have difficulty with reading and writing.

The Lesson

I wrote the weekly vocabulary from our "New Word List" from the preceding classes on separate pieces of cardboard, one word per piece. I used a different colored marker for each grammatical function, red for the subjects, green for the verbs, and purple for the statements that could end the sentence. Each category had about 15 to 20 selections.

Next, I put the pieces of cardboard on the floor—placing all the subjects in the first column, the verbs in the next, followed by a third column of statements that could complete the sentence. I invited the students to make a sentence by leaping from subject to verb to ending. One point was given for each correct sentence. The students and I determined whether the sentences were correct by discussing each one after it had been formed.

We usually played this game in two teams. The students chose the order of the players, and they kept track of the score. I allowed my students to go back and start over if they were stuck, but you could implement a "no going back" rule, if you so desired.

Reflections and Student Responses

The class really liked to play this game. Having students jump between words not only adds an element of challenge but also seems to help them to remember the word order as they move from the subject, through the verb, to the appropriate ending.

The group process is also an important aspect of this activity. In my class, students experimented with possible word combinations, discussing their choices aloud, coaching each other, and sharing their collective knowledge.

— Learning English Through Movement: Obstacle Course —

Terri Coustan

Terri developed this ESOL lesson to tap into her students' bodily-kinesthetic intelligence.

Subject   Language arts
Curriculum Objective
            Giving and following directions
Time   20 minutes
Materials   Rulers, large pieces of paper, pencils, erasers, and any other objects you have on hand

Background

I teach in a family literacy program in which 17 parents come to school with their 12 preschool-aged children. The students are between the ages of 30 and 50. Most of the students in the class are Hmong from the hills of Laos. Some are struggling to communicate orally in English, whereas others have difficulty with reading and writing.

Because this game involves trust, you may want to wait to use it until a time when the students are comfortable with each other.

The Lesson

Using rulers to mark the perimeter, I created a 15- by 20-foot obstacle course on the floor. I filled the middle with crayons and erasers and any other objects that I had readily available. Before I began the course, I reviewed any appropriate vocabulary, including directional words, left and right, adjectives, and verbs.

I introduced the activity by telling my students that this area represented a "garden" filled with "snakes" (the crayons and erasers) and "plants," "vegetables," and "fences" (the other objects). Their objective was to walk blindfolded through the field while avoiding the "snakes" and other obstacles. A partner provided verbal cues from outside the perimeter of the course. (Examples: "Take a little step forward." "Turn to the right.") One member of the class went at a time.

I used this game in my family literacy class and had the children guide their parents through the course to the finish line.

Reflections and Student Responses

The students seemed to learn more easily and quickly as they moved around the course. Even the quietest student participated and found a way to verbally communicate the necessary directions to her teammate. The activity also built trust and helped develop a bond between the students.

Obstacle Course was great for reinforcing directional words. Even the students who were confident that they knew left and right had difficulty executing these terms in the game.

Although I used the game as part of my Indoor Gardening unit, it could be adapted to work with any theme.

MI-inspired Math and Science Lessons

— Dish It Out: Subtracting With Beans and Plates —

Betsy Cornwell

This activity draws on students' spatial intelligence to learn subtraction.

> Students were having a hard time understanding place value, so we decided to use the Beans and Plates lesson. The students did very well with the lesson. Most of the students understood and gained a lot of understanding from the lesson. I did have a few students who thought it was boring and felt they learned better the traditional way. I reminded the students that, as we had discussed before we started the MI project, because we all used different intelligences depending on our own style of learning, we might differ from each other in liking or disliking some of the activities.
> ~ Rebecca Martin, AMI Sourcebook Pilot Teacher

Subject   Math
Curriculum Objective
          To learn subtraction with large numbers
Time   30 minutes
Materials   1 pound or more of dried beans; 10 to 20 small paper dessert plates; marker; work sheet with subtraction problems involving numbers larger than 10,000; scratch paper; pencil

Background

I used this math activity with my ABE students who had trouble learning math using just paper-and-pencil.

The Lesson

Step 1

Select a subtraction problem and ask the student to read it, ensuring that numbers are expressed correctly. Example:

$$\begin{array}{r} 23,435 \\ -19,876 \\ \hline \end{array}$$

Step 2

Place a plate in front of your student and ask him or her to put 23,435 beans on it. Listen carefully to the response because you will be given important clues regarding your student's understanding of large numbers. If your student wants to count all the beans, I think that might be a good idea because it will give him or her a better idea of what "23,435" means. Allow your student to go as far as he or she can toward expressing "23,435" with the beans. If your student is unable to come up with a reasonable expression, go to step 3.

Step 3

Place five plates on the table and write place names with the marker according to Figure 4.1.

Figure 4.1. Dish It Out Plates

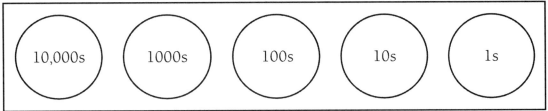

The number can now be expressed by placing two beans in the "10,000s" plate, three beans in the "1000s" plate and so on, as in Figure 4.2.

Figure 4.2. Dish It Out Plates With Beans (Start)

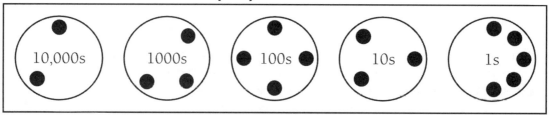

Have your student practice expressing numbers on plates until he or she is comfortable with the system. As your student places beans into plates, insist that he or she count by the number on the plate. For example, when placing five beans in the "1s" plate, the student will say, "One, two, three, four, five." When placing three beans in the "10s" plate, he or she will say, "Ten, twenty, thirty," and so on.

Step 4

Refer back to the original problem and ask your student to remove 19,876 beans from the plates. As the student tries to decide how to do this, you may need to remind him or her that each individual bean stands for the number written on the plate (e.g., each bean on the "100s" plate stands for 100 beans). If your student objects that "there aren't enough beans on the '1s' plate," you may be able to help things along by asking where he or she might be able to get more beans for the "1s" plate. When the student picks up a bean from the "10s" plate, observe that he or she is holding ten beans. When the student removes one bean from the "10s" plate, he or she will need to put ten beans on the "1s" plate. This process will be simpler if you always remember to count by 10s when counting the beans on the "10s" plate.

Step 5

When you're finished, your plates should look like those shown in Figure 4.3. Ask your student what number is represented and how he or she would know if the answer were correct. The student could check his or her work by adding "19,876" beans back onto the plates, doing the problem with a calculator, reproducing it on paper, or looking in the back of the book for answers. The important thing is that the student feels comfortable with the accuracy of the process.

Figure 4.3. Dish It Out Plates With Beans (Finish)

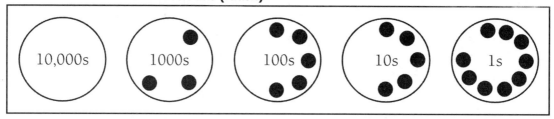

Step 6

Once your student feels comfortable with the beans and plates subtraction process, ask him or her to record each step on paper. The beans and plates take up space and using them is time consuming. You'll know your student is ready to graduate to subtracting on paper when he or she no longer wants to bother with beans.

Reflections and Student Responses

When Beth, Ben, and I designed this lesson, we had plates, beans, markers, and a work sheet of subtraction problems on the table in front of us. We fooled around with the materials until we came up with a helpful procedure. I find that putting the process into writing is a whole different ball game. What looks complicated on paper was much simpler when we were experimenting with actual beans.

This process works only for some students. Beth wasn't impressed with it. She said subtracting on paper was much easier. Ben, on the other hand, said it helped him. He came back to the beans and plates for several sessions until the concept of place values began to seem less arbitrary and abstract to him. Now he prefers to subtract on paper and does so with a reasonable degree of accuracy.

— Backdoor Algebra —

Meg Costanzo

Meg developed this lesson to help her students solve math problems with variables. It draws on students' spatial intelligence as a way to learn basic algebra.

Subject   Math
Curriculum Objective
            To solve problems with variables
Materials   Paper plates, in assorted colors; bag of dried beans; package of 5- by 8-inch index cards;
            student math journals

Background

To help my GED students overcome their reluctance to solve these types of math problems, I recommend using the backdoor approach to teaching algebra described below. This approach helps eliminate the fear and anxiety that often holds the students back from attempting to solve problems containing unknowns.

The Lesson

Begin by modeling this technique for the students. For students who have little experience solving problems containing variables, I recommend starting with a very basic problem, such as $4y = 20$. Explain that the 4 in this problem stands for four groups of the same amount "y." Tell the students that they are solving for the value of y.

Place four paper plates, all the same color, in front of the students. Upon each plate, place an index card on which the letter y has been written. Tell the students that these plates represent $4y$. Then place an index card with an equal sign such that it appears, from the students' vantage, to the right of the four plates. Lastly, place a different colored plate to the right of this symbol. Refer back to the problem. Ask the students to guess what might be found on this final plate. Once the students have determined 20, place an index card with this number written on it on the plate. Then count out 20 beans and put them on top of this plate.

Have the students figure out how many beans need to go on each of the four plates to equal 20. Remind the students that each plate must contain the same number of beans. Encourage the students to redistribute the 20 beans to help solve this problem. Once the students have completed this task, demonstrate how this problem can be solved mathematically. Relate what the students did to rearrange the beans to this mathematical process.

$$4y = 20$$

$$\frac{4y}{4} = \frac{20}{4}$$

$$y = 5$$

Once the students have demonstrated an understanding of how to solve a variety of simple algebraic equations, move on to more difficult problems, such as $3x + 2 = 14$. Explain that the 3 found in the problem $3x + 2 = 14$ stands for three groups of "x." Place three paper plates of the same color on the table. Upon each plate, place an index card on which the letter x has been written.

Then write a plus sign on another index card and place it so, from the students' vantage point, it appears to the right of the plates. Next to that, place a different colored paper plate and set an index card with the number 2 on that plate. Point out how the number 2 relates to the problem they are solving.

Then put out another index card with an equal sign and a paper plate of a third color. Ask the students what they might expect to find on the third plate. After eliciting their responses, place the number 14 and 14 beans on the last plate.

Explain to the students that this math lesson is going to be different from the others they have just experienced. Instead of solving to find the value of x, they will be given the answer, $x = 4$, up front. Their assignment is to come up with a way to prove that answer is indeed correct. Encourage the students to brainstorm various ways they might accomplish this.

After the students have finished with this part of the assignment, explain the step-by-step mathematical procedure for solving this kind of problem and, as you review each step, correlate it to what the students did when proving this answer.

$$3x + 2 = 14$$
$$-2 = -2$$
$$3x + 0 = 12$$
$$\frac{3x}{3} = \frac{12}{3}$$
$$x = 4$$

As the students become more comfortable solving problems this way, have them work independently, in pairs or in small groups, to solve increasingly difficult algebra problems that are presented in the following format.

On one side of a 5- by 8-inch index card, print a problem. For example,

If $2x + 3y = 19$ and $x = 2$, what is the value of y?

On the reverse side of the card, show how the problem can be solved.

$$2x + 3y = 19$$
$$(2 \times 2) + 3y = 19$$
$$4 + 3y = 19$$
$$-4 \quad = -4$$
$$0 + 3y = 15$$
$$\frac{3y}{3} = \frac{15}{3}$$
$$y = 5$$

Give the students a choice in how they approach this assignment. Those students who feel they know how to perform a mathematical solution to the problem can simply solve the problem and check their answers by looking on the reverse side of the card. Those who are uncertain about how to proceed can begin by looking at the solution, then designing a way to prove that the given answer is correct. As the students become more confident in solving these types of problems, encourage them to attempt the mathematical solutions first. Keep these problems and materials on hand so students have the opportunity to review these skills whenever they wish.

As the students solve these problems, have them record the results of their work in their math journals. Keeping MI theory in mind, encourage students to develop their own individual methods for recording their responses. Those students who feel more comfortable writing a mathematical solution should opt to record their work in a traditional math format (see above). Those who are more comfortable with writing their solutions in paragraph or list form should present their work in this format. Those who would prefer to include drawings or diagrams should pursue this approach. In many cases, students may develop their own unique ways of recording their work that reflect a combination of their intelligence strengths.

Reflections and Student Responses

I found that one of the most interesting results of my work with the AMI Study was the way it transformed my thinking as a teacher. In the past, when faced with a challenge like the one involving my students' reaction to variables in an equation, I would have asked myself, "How can I teach this skill more effectively?" Now I find myself asking, "How can my knowledge of MI theory influence how I facilitate learning in my classroom?" or "How can I encourage my students to use their strongest intelligences to learn this skill?" I look for ways to have my students create "products" that demonstrate their understanding of the skills being taught. In the case of the backdoor algebra assignments, the products are the various approaches the students employed when solving the problems and the math journal entries that describe their work.

Extensions

Have the students write word problems to accompany the equations they have solved.

$4y = 20$

One week, Theresa worked 4 days for a total of 20 hours. If she worked an equal number of hours each day, how many hours did she work on any given workday that week?

$3x + 2 = 14$

Rob has 14 photographs. After he finishes putting them in his album, he has filled three full pages and has two photos left over. If he put an equal number of photos on each page, how many photos can be found on each?

— Choose 3: Angles —

Martha Jean

This lesson is an example of the Choose 3 format applied to math Martha developed. For a fuller description of Martha's class and the Choose 3 approach, please see Martha's write-up under MI Lesson Formats earlier in this chapter.

Angles

Here's my goal;
now, here's the aim:
Not all angles are the same.
If you want me feeling fine,
What you've got to do is cross two lines.
I won't argue; I won't fight,
Ninety degrees is always "right."
Now listen up;
here's the plan:
For an "obtuse" angle, picture a fan.
Spread it open
but not too far—
ninety to one-eighty,
you'll be a star!
Less than ninety,
you can make a "beaut";
Just remember,
it's called "acute."
Finally one more,
but don't be vexed.
Over one-eighty is called "reflex."
      ~ Dave Berman, participant in an AMI workshop Angles activity

Subject   Math
Curriculum Objective
          To review the concept of angles
Materials   Paper, pencil, pens, rulers, protractors, paint, Play-Doh®

Background

I teach GED. I wanted to find a way to expand the number of learning activities that my students could experience while still preparing for the five GED exams. I was especially concerned with helping those students who experience learning difficulties.

In a previous class, my GED students had talked about and looked at 360°, 180°, 90°, and 45° angles. They had practiced naming angles and using a protractor. They made triangles out of long strips of thin paper.

The Lesson

1.   In 2 to 5 minutes, list as many angles as you can find outside the class—acute, right, obtuse, and straight.

    a.   Count the number of each type of angle and make a graph showing each type that you found.

    b.   Which angle is most common? Why?

2.   Use your arm and elbow to form five angles.

    a.   Draw those angles and write approximate measures for each.

    b.   Are there any kinds of angles that cannot be made with an elbow? Explain your answer.

3.   Discuss with someone and write responses to these questions:

    a.   What does someone mean when he or she says, "What's your angle?"

    b.   If you were on an icy road and did a "360," what happened to you?

    c.   Why do you think the shape L is called a right angle?

4.   Using Play-Doh® and/or paper, show the angles 180°, 135°, 90°, and 45°.

5.   Find or make five triangles. Measure each angle and find the total number of degrees in each triangle by adding up the sums of the three angles.

6.   Draw, make with Play-Doh®, or paint a place you know. Mark and measure the angles in your design.

7.   Write a poem, song, chant, or rap using some of the following words about angles:

    o   figure formed by two lines, intersection, elbow, notch, cusp, fork, flare, obtuse, acute

    o   point of view, perspective, viewpoint, outlook, slant, standpoint, position

    o   purpose, intention, plan, aim, objective, approach, method

Reflections and Student Responses

This was one of the first choice lessons that I designed around a single idea. The focus in this Angles lesson meant that I was more certain that each student had reviewed that specific concept.

— Choose 3: Measurement —

Martha Jean

This lesson is an example of the Choose 3 format applied to math Martha developed. For a fuller description of Martha's class and the Choose 3 approach, please see Martha's write-up under MI Lesson Formats earlier in this chapter.

Subject Math
Curriculum Objective
            To review how to multiply and divide measurements
Materials Paper, pencil, pens, rulers, measuring spoons, water, funnel, containers, string, protractors, paint, Play-Doh®

Background

I teach GED. I wanted to find a way to expand the number of learning activities that my students could experience while still preparing for the five GED exams. I was especially concerned with helping those students who experience learning difficulties.

The Lesson

1. On strips of paper, measure out and cut 12 one-inch pieces, 3 twelve-inch (one-foot) pieces, and 1 thirty-six-inch (one yard) piece. Put the smaller pieces together until they equal the next larger measure.

2. Use measuring spoons to answer these questions: If you put 3 teaspoons of Play-Doh® together, what other measure does that equal? If you cut 1 teaspoon of Play-Doh® into four equal pieces, how much is one of those parts? If you cut 1 teaspoon into two equal parts, how much is one of those parts? If you put the two parts back together, what do they equal?

3. Using water, the funnel, and containers, show how 2 cups equal a pint, 2 pints equal a quart, and 4 quarts equal a gallon.

4. Make strips of paper or pieces of string the length of your body, arm, and hand. Measure each of the strips or pieces of string.

5. Make a graph of the heights of everyone in the classroom or the estimated heights of five people you know.

6. Draw a picture of a few of the tallest and the shortest things familiar to you. Estimate their heights.

7. Write a story about a time that you followed a recipe to make something new. Include measurements (exact or estimates) and how it all turned out.

8. Think music! How many $1/4$ rests do you think have the same value as a whole rest? How many $1/2$ rests equal a whole rest? How many $1/4$ rests have the same value as a $1/2$ rest?

9. Work with another person or a group to list the things you might measure at home or at work. Which instrument (ruler, cup, spoon, and so on) would you use to measure each of them?

10. Write a story, poem, song, or chant about a time when you measured up to your own expectations.

— Choose 3: Time Zones: Are You in the Zone? —

Martha Jean

This lesson is an example of Choose 3 format applied to math Martha developed. For a fuller description of Martha's class and the Choose 3 approach, please see Martha's write-up under MI Lesson Formats earlier in this chapter.

Subject   Science
Curriculum Objective
                To learn the concept of time zones
Materials   Paper, pencils, pens, markers, U.S. reference maps, blank U.S. maps, packet of GED time
                zone questions

Background

I teach GED. I wanted to find a way to expand the number of learning activities that my students could experience while still preparing for the five GED exams. I was especially concerned with helping those students who experience learning difficulties.

The Lesson

The class started with a "walk" across the time zones. I had used wide strips of black paper to mark on the floor four areas representing the major time zones in the United States. I taped a big, yellow paper "sun" to the window. First, I explained that we were going to start in the Eastern Time Zone with the sun rising at 5:00 a.m. Then we walked into the Central Time Zone, where I said it was 4:00 a.m. and the sun wasn't up yet. We continued across the Mountain Time Zone and into the Pacific Time Zone; as we moved, I asked questions about the time changes that would be taking place. We stopped in each zone and talked about where we were in relation to the other zones and where the sun would be situated. Then I asked them what time it would be in the Mountain, Central, and Eastern time zones if it were 8:00 p.m. in the Pacific Time Zone. After they completed that task, I knew they were ready for the Choose 3 Activity.

Choose 3 Activity

1. On a blank U.S. map, outline or color in the Eastern, Central, Mountain, and Pacific time zones.

2. On a blank U.S. map, write in as many state names as you can remember, and then use a reference map to help you fill in the rest.

3. Show on a time zone map what time it is in each time zone when you wake up, eat lunch, eat supper, and go to sleep.

4. Write in what ways the geographic area in each time zone is different from that in the others.

5. Pick one city or town from each time zone and write about the type of music that you think is popular in each one.

6. Using an imaginary floor map, walk down each time zone line and name the states you would pass through or see on either side of the border.

7. Look at the GED questions in the packet. On your blank map, write in the names of the cities that are mentioned.

8. Rate the four U.S. time zones from your favorite to your least favorite zone. Write why you feel that way about each one.

9. Do a class survey. Ask each person which is their favorite and least favorite time zone and why. Write or graph the results.

Postactivity Work

1. I assigned the students GED workbook time zone questions.

2. I had the students play the board game called "Travel USA" with their fellow classmates. (In this commercially made game, players go up and down a grid on a map of the United States, landing on question card sites pertaining to states, capitals, products, and distances.)

3. I divided the class into two teams that played a teacher-made "Jeopardy!"-type game with these categories: "State Shapes," "Ocean or Country View?" "City in Which State?" "Distances between Cities," and "City in Which Time Zone?" Have three different values for the questions: $50 (easy), $100 (less easy), and $200 (hard). We followed the rules for the TV game.

Reflections and Student Responses

After this round of Choose 3 activities, another benefit of this lesson format became evident: its role as a diagnostic tool. As a result of student performance on these tasks, I was able to recognize the need to review the locations of U.S. cities and states with the class.

After working on this Choose 3 activity, most students got all the GED workbook time zone questions correct. In the activities that followed, students also had excellent time zone information recall.

— Math Review Card Game —

Meg Costanzo

Meg took the idea of Wendy's Parts-of-Speech Trading Cards game and created this math review activity for her students.

Subject   Math
Curriculum Objective
             To review decimals, percentages, fractions, and measurements
Materials Packages of 3- by 5-inch index cards (I used three different colors)
             Fine line markers
             Instruction sheet for each student
             Rulers, measuring cups, showing cups, pints and quarts, gallon containers, fraction pieces, and any other appropriate math manipulatives that coordinate with the skills being reviewed
             Math workbooks

Background

I developed this game to help the students who were enrolled in our GED/Adult Diploma program review the information they needed to know in order to pass the math portion of their exam.

The Lesson

I made sets of index cards, each containing three pieces of math information that were somehow related. For instance, I had three cards showing different ways to name 1 gallon (4 quarts, 8 pints) and $1/2$ (0.5 and 50%). I divided the cards into two main categories: "measurement and fractions," "decimals and percentages." There were about 12 to 15 sets of cards for each category. On some of the cards, I had pictures to represent the information being emphasized; for instance, one card showed a circle divided into four equal parts, with three of the four parts shaded (three fourths); another showed a line segment that was 3 inches long ($1/4$ foot).

I placed the appropriate manipulatives in the center of the table and dealt out the cards from one of the categories (face down) such that each student received about the same number of cards.

I then told the students that I was going to give them a very basic introduction to this activity, but, after that, they were on their own in figuring out how to go about following the directions. Without saying anything else, I placed the three cards showing $1/2$, 0.5, and 50% together to form a set.

After passing out the instruction sheets, which the students read on their own, I told them they could begin working. I stood back and observed how they interacted as they tried to carry out the directions. I did not intervene unless it became necessary. Following the directions, the students let me know when they were finished.

Student Directions

The object of this review lesson is to find sets, or related groups, of math information. When you are done, each set should contain three cards that show information that somehow belongs together. For example, the cards $1/2$, 0.5, and 50% would go together to form a set because they all name the same part of a whole.

You will be given different cards. In some cases, you may have the beginning of a set already. That is, you may have the two cards showing $1/2$ and 50%. You then will have to ask someone else in the class if he or she has a card that shows another way of expressing $1/2$ and 50%. Cards can be traded freely at any time.

Sometimes, you may not have any cards that go together at first. Just keep trading cards until all the cards have been placed into sets. The review lesson is over when all the cards are in sets of three and everyone agrees that all the sets are accurately matched. This is a team activity, not a competition.

There are materials on the table for you to use when forming the sets. However, to make this more of a challenge, you may consult your notes or workbook only when, after a team conference, you cannot agree on an answer.

Have fun with this. Remember to trust your different intelligences!

Postactivity Questions

1. Which sets were easy to form?
2. Which ones gave you more difficulty?
3. In which areas, if any, do you feel you need more work?

When I had originally made up the sets of three cards, I put each related fact on a different colored index card. After the students finished the activity, I asked them if they saw any pattern to how the sets were arranged.

Reflections and Student Responses

This game gave me the opportunity to observe my students in a cooperative setting using their strongest intelligences.

I was pleased with how the students responded to the game. They helped one another, frequently giving little "minilessons" to prove their points. The following quote tells of one student's reaction to the activity: "Meg came into the room and announced our assignment was going to be a math review. The sudden look of death overcame us.... In a joint effort, we had all the cards matched in a very short period of time. The surprise assignment turned into a learning activity that we had fun doing!"

Extensions

o   Have the students make up a fourth card that could fit with each set.

o   Ask the students to complete this activity without speaking to one another.

o   Include extra cards in the mix that do not belong with the sets. Tell the students ahead of time that some cards may be left over when they are done.

o   Have the students make up an activity similar to this one. Other subject matter lends itself to this kind of review.

o   After the students have played the game as a group, have each one use the cards independently as further review of the material.

— Edible Math: Volume in the Real World —

Betsy Cornwell

Experimentation and discovery are the focus of this math lesson.

Subject   Math
Curriculum Objective
            To learn graphing, weighing, estimating, multiplying, dividing, and computing volume
Time   1 hour
Materials Three or more bags of potato chips, different brands. (If prices are not marked on the
            packages, write them on the packages or provide supermarket receipts.)
            Small scale (for weighing ounces)
            Plastic boxes or bowls for serving/storing potato chips
            Graph paper, plain paper, blackboard or chart paper, pens, pencils, crayons, colored
            chalk. (Try to provide students with a variety of materials for them to use while docu-
            menting their process and findings.)
            List of questions regarding the bags of chips (or students may supply questions)
            Paper napkins and water or other beverages. (Sampling the results of the exploration can
            induce thirst!)

Background

I taught this lesson to my ABE students. This lesson works best with small groups. This could
be an especially useful activity for a new group, giving students and teacher an opportunity to become familiar with each other's problem-solving strategies and maybe their underlying intelligences.

The Lesson

I began the lesson by displaying the potato chips and materials at the front of the room. I asked
the students to examine the bags of potato chips and brainstorm questions about them. I told the
students that they would be exploring the answers to these questions later. Part of the fun of this
lesson was the "junk-food-inspired" spontaneity. I wrote down every question I heard. Once they realized that they would need to research real answers to at least some of the questions, the students
were usually eager to point out the frivolousness of some of the questions and come up with better
ones. Some of the questions we generated included the following:

o   Which bag is the best buy? (How does one define "best buy"?)

o   Which brand has less fat?

o   How many chips in a serving? Is it the same for all brands?

o   Which brand tastes best? How could we define "tastes best"? How could we represent the
     various taste preferences of group members?

o   How far would I have to walk to burn off the calories from one serving of "Brand X"?

o   Why do these two bags claim to weigh the same, yet one is bigger?

I then asked each group to choose a question to answer. They had to decide on the materials
they would need, research their answer, and share their results with the rest of the class. When I had
only one group, they had to share their results with a neighboring class, prepare an artifact for their
portfolios, or write a brief description of the project for a newsletter or journal.

The group members came up with clever ways to share their findings. Depending on the chosen
question, the answers took the form of skits, graphs, demonstrations, or blow-by-blow descriptions
of the problem-solving process. Finally, the other students and I asked each group questions about
their research process and their results.

Reflections and Student Responses

I think that having the students share their answers is an important part of the process. Explaining an experience takes the student from merely understanding a concept to being able to express it clearly. Having a real audience created an inescapable need to communicate effectively.

One of the reasons I liked this lesson so much is that it effectively put people at ease. In the past, I've had many students who suffer from "math anxiety," but I have yet to encounter someone with "potato chip anxiety." For example, one of my students was typically cooperative but very passive when we did math. When she saw my bags of chips, she immediately wanted to know why the 6-ounce bag was larger than the 8-ounce bag. She got busy comparing labels, weighing chips, and pouring them into boxes right away.

Extensions

o   During student presentations, ask which intelligences the students observe at work.

o   Have each group write up the results of their project as a multiple-choice word problem. This will take time and might work best as a follow-up class.

o   Videotape the presentations, or take step-by-step pictures. Show the tape or pictures at a later lesson, and ask students to talk or write about what happened.

— Choose 3: Science Lessons, Matter and Mitosis —

Ivy Dominick

Ivy learned about the MI-based Choose 3 lesson format from Judy Hickey, one of the AMI Sourcebook Pilot Teachers, and applied it to her science lessons to tap into more of her students' intelligences.

Subject   Science
Curriculum Objectives
            To apply understanding of the concept of physical and chemical changes
            To apply understanding of the concept of cells and mitosis
Time   Two or three 60-minute class periods of formal instruction in a specific subject area, plus one 60-minute class period devoted to Choose 3 activities.
Materials Matter: Physical and Chemical Changes: displays showing various examples of physical and chemical changes; drawing paper; markers; sugar; salt; glass containers; gumdrops; miniature marshmallows; toothpicks; glue
            Cells and Mitosis: drawing paper, markers, assorted materials for constructing cell models, including beans, bits of pasta, string, cardboard, and the ingredients for salt dough

Background

When I first heard about the Choose 3 lesson format, I thought to myself, "I wish my teachers had given me choices like these when I was in school." Although I had always incorporated demonstrations and hands-on activities into my lessons, I had never offered the students any choice in how they could demonstrate their knowledge of the topics we studied. These new assignments seemed like magic to me. I consider myself a creative teacher, but this format presented me with an even wider range of ways to stimulate my students' interest in science.

I teach several different classes at The Learning Bank. My diverse groups range from basic skills classes, with students reading at either third- or fifth-grade level, to GED prep classes in which students function at an eighth- to tenth-grade reading level. My students all follow the same curriculum regardless of the class they attend.

I am able to teach sophisticated topics to all levels of learners by tailoring the reading material that I present to each class. Using standard texts, information off the Internet, and my own knowledge of scientific topics acquired while studying premed, I often rewrite materials in order to reach students who are functioning on a lower reading level than the rest. Some science words cannot be simplified, so instead they are explained in a simpler way. Even my lowest level class will still be exposed to a word like neuropsychopharmacology, but only after I've taught a few lessons about neurons and the central nervous system. The students recognize how words from their own vocabulary, like *psycho* and *pharmacy,* relate to this word. They are very proud when they realize they now have the ability to translate lengthy scientific terms.

Before assigning the Choose 3 activities, we spent two or three class periods learning about the topic through discussion, demonstration, and reading from the appropriate materials. Then all students, regardless of ability level, got to select from the same list of Choose 3 assignments.

Matter: Physical and Chemical Changes Activity

1.   Look around the room. Can you find any substances that have undergone a chemical or physical change? List as many as you can for each category.
2.   Be molecules! Hold pieces of paper that show the symbols for the atoms you represent. Interact with other molecules to show what happens during a chemical reaction or a physical change.
3.   Draw a diagram that depicts a substance in its various stages.
4.   Time how long it takes for 3 tablespoons of sugar or salt to dissolve in
      a.   cold water

    b. tepid water

    c. hot water

Record the times in chart form. If possible, find a group that has dissolved a substance different from yours. Compare and contrast the information on the two charts. What might explain any similarities? Discrepancies?

5. Using gumdrops, marshmallows, and toothpicks, build models that represent a chemical reaction that we have studied in class. Show both the unreacted molecule before the chemical reaction has taken place and the new molecule that is formed as a result of that reaction.

6. Make a collage showing various materials undergoing chemical and physical changes. Explain your selection of pictures to the class.

7. Present to the class a demonstration of either a chemical or physical change.

8. Write a poem or song about a chemical or physical change.

9. Brainstorm a list of the physical and chemical changes that occur in our everyday lives from morning to night.

Cells and Mitosis Activity

1. Draw and label the parts of any type of cell: plant, animal, or bacterial. Write down the function of each organelle next to its label.

2. In a group of four people, plan and perform a skit that demonstrates how a cell makes proteins. Assign one person to each of these roles: DNA, Ribosomes, Smooth or Rough ER, and Golgi Complex.

3. In a small group, act out the process of mitosis. Demonstrate how duplicated DNA meets in the middle during metaphase and separates during anaphase.

4. Write a song, rap, or poem about the cell and/or mitosis.

5. What would happen to a cell if it did not have mitochondria? Vacuoles? DNA? Membrane? Any other organelle? Write down your answers.

6. Pretend you are a cell that is missing one of its organelles. How would you feel? How would you act? (If you are having trouble completing this activity, I suggest doing #5 first.) Plan a way to present your responses to the class.

7. Build a model of a cell using any set of materials you wish. See me for the recipe for salt dough.

8. Draw and label the stages of mitosis. Below each stage, write an explanation of what is happening.

9. Pretend that you are a medical professional talking to someone who has recently been diagnosed with cancer. This patient has no knowledge of what causes cancer and wants to know what is happening. What would you say, and how would you say it?

10. Design an advertisement or poster informing others about cancer prevention.

11. Write a song or poem about cancer and its prevention. If someone close to you has or had cancer, write a tribute to him or her.

12. Teach the class about the five stages of mitosis. Use any visual aids that you wish.

Reflections and Student Responses

For the most part, students responded very positively to the Choose 3 assignments. I heard comments like, "I never thought I could understand chemistry," or "I never thought I could learn physics." The biggest problem that I experienced using this format arose when students had been absent for the preliminary class work. Understandably, I found that these students had difficulty catching up to a point where they could produce quality projects within the constraints of the time available.

I also found that sometimes it was preferable to have the students complete only two of the activities. I realized that it was more beneficial to have them do two activities that represented their best efforts rather than rush through their work to finish a third assignment. Depending on the class, the topic we are studying, or the time available to us, future Choose 3 activities might be revised to Select 2!

MI-inspired Thematic Units

— Coming to America I —

Terri Couslan

Terri framed these units around real-life stories that had been written by her beginning level ESOL students.

Subject   Language arts, vocabulary, and reading
Curriculum Objective
        To develop vocabulary, reading, and writing
Time   About 12 hours

Background

I teach in a family literacy program in which 17 parents come to school with their 12 preschool-aged children. Most of the students in the class are Hmong from the hills of Laos. Some are struggling to communicate orally in English, whereas others have difficulty with reading and writing.

I emphasize the natural vocabulary of the students and use MI-based instruction to encourage students to use their own words in writing stories about topics of importance to them.

I did this activity every week, modeled after Martha Jean's Choose 3 idea. The activities varied from week to week. I also tried to provide opportunities for the students to draw upon their different intelligences when completing the Choose 3 selections. The students told me that it was "fun" to do these "new things."

Lesson 1

Materials   Video from *Hmong Tapestry Curriculum,* produced by the Hmong American Partnership, 450 North Syndicate, Suite 35, St. Paul, MN 55104 (612-642-9601), 1992
        Picture of a family leaving Thailand and arriving in America, *Hmong in America: Journey From a Secret War,* Tim Pfaff, Chippewa Valley Museum Press, 1995
        Chart paper
        Copies of poem/story from the video clip
        Play-Doh® and Lite-Brite®

Video Clip Part 1

I introduced the class to the theme of Coming to America by way of a short clip from the video *Tapestry*. High school age Hmong students now living in Minnesota produced this video. It is a play based on a re-creation of the war and the subsequent journey of the Hmong to America. The dialogue is in Hmong and English. The first clip involves the reading of a poem or song by the students in full Hmong costume. The poem describes the Hmong's will and ability to survive through the worst of times.

I listened to my students as they talked while watching the video. They commented on the music and the costumes. The musical instruments reminded them of their mothers and fathers. There were sighs and tears.

Story/Poem

I gave everyone a copy of the story/poem that was read in the video clip. We then read it together and discussed the words in the poem. I gave the students time to reflect on the words and to collect their thoughts after such an emotional video. Students in the class from other cultures shared common thoughts about their struggles and their will to survive.

Video Clip Part 2

In the second video clip (5 minutes), the actors depict the Hmong leaving the Thai refugee camp. They are shown carrying their suitcases for the trip to America. The scene is filled with the sobbing of relatives as they say their last goodbyes.

Class Discussion

I asked the class (10 minutes) what they had seen. I asked them if something similar had happened to them and how they had felt. They shared stories about leaving their families in Laos, the Dominican Republic, and Ghana. We also talked about going home. We discussed the length of the airplane trip, the price of a ticket, and the locations of their homelands on a map. I wrote key words on the blackboard.

Photo Story

I passed out a picture of a Hmong family with few possessions arriving at an airport in the United States. I asked the class to help me write a story. At the bottom of the picture were the following questions to help the students frame the story: What do you see? What is the problem? Did this ever happen to you? As the students spoke, I recorded their words on chart paper.

As a class, we reread the story we had just written. I asked the class to tell me the words that were new to them, words that they couldn't read, or words that they would have difficulty writing. These words formed a "New Word List." I posted the list on the wall for the entire week, along with our weekly story, to serve as reference points for the class.

The students asked to copy the story. Those who finished reread the story to me. When the students finished reading, they identified their new words from the story. These words were listed on chart paper. As one of the class activities, I invited the students to form the vocabulary from this list into words made from Play-Doh® or create them using Lite-Brite®. Students participated in all of these activities.

Video Goes Home

I asked who wanted to take the video home to share with family members. Because everyone wanted to do this, we created a schedule with a list of names.

Lesson 2

Materials Pandau (a Hmong wall hanging), paper, *National Geographic* magazines, scissors, and glue

Viewing a Pandau

I brought in a pandau that showed soldiers carrying the Hmong flag in a declaration of freedom. We tried to translate the Laotian words that were written on it. We talked about the flag shown on the hanging, as well as the flags of Ghana and the United States.

Computer Work

I gave each student a typed copy of the previous day's story. It included a picture of the Hmong coming to America. Each student retyped the story onto his or her own disk. The students made two copies of the story. One was for my work folder, the other for the student's individual work folder.

New Word Study

I asked the students to demonstrate that they understood one word from the "New Word List." I suggested that they could draw a picture about the word, use it in a sentence, cut out a picture showing the word, or try something else. For example, for the word *house,* one student used the idea of this word in a sentence— "I live at 120 Brown St." Others wrote the word in Hmong.

Lesson 3

Materials Scissors and glue

Story cut up sentence by sentence

Cloze exercise (This is a copy of our authentic story with words left out so that the students can fill in the blanks.)

LEGO® bricks

Glitter and colored sand

Work sheet with the new vocabulary words in scrambled form

Choose 3 list of activities

Choose 3 Activities

I handed the class a list of activities that involved the story of the week. As I described each activity, I told the students to choose three activities by putting a check next to those that they wanted to do. I carefully described each activity along with the materials that would be needed to complete the activity. At the completion of the explanation, they got the materials they would need and began to work on their chosen activities. As the students were engaged in their work, I took a photo of each of the students to be used in a photo journal on the following day. The Choose 3 activities gave me, as well as the students, a chance to discover their intelligences. I observed what they chose and how engaged they were in the activities. This information helped me plan for the next week's Choose 3 activities.

Choices

o Put the cut-up story strips in sequential order.

o Draw a picture of people coming to America.

o Cut out pictures from a magazine showing people coming to America.

o Write a story about your trip to America.

o Show people coming to America in Play-Doh® or LEGO® bricks.

o Put words in the story.

o Tell me about the problems of coming to America.

o Find a picture of a woman crying.

o Unscramble the words on your "New Words" work sheet.

o Make your "New Words" in glitter and sand.

Lesson 4

Materials Photos from Day 3, pasted in students' journals; story sentences cut up and placed in envelopes

Photo Journal

At the beginning of the class, I distributed the photo journals to each student. The first page of each journal contained a photo of the student engaged in one of the previous day's Choose 3 activities. Along with the photo, I included three questions:

1. What are you doing in the photo?

2. Did you like the activity?

3. Would you like to do this activity again?

The students' photo journals served as logs of the activities they had tried and their thoughts about the activities. I encouraged the students to work in any way that was comfortable for them. Some students worked independently on the photo journals; others worked in pairs; others with little proficiency in English asked me to write their thoughts on the blackboard for them to copy. Because a Hmong translator was available that day, she helped those students who were more comfortable speaking in Hmong.

Spelling Dictation Activity

I dictated simple sentences using the natural vocabulary of the students as much as possible; for example, "I came on a boat." The class worked as one big group to write the sentences. I gave them as much time as they needed to write their answers. I collected the papers, reviewed them, and returned them with the rest of the week's work on Monday.

I divided the blackboard into sections—one space for each of the dictated sentences. I asked volunteers to write their dictations on the blackboard. The students and I helped to correct the work.

Dramatization of the Story

After we read the story as a class, I cut the story into sentence strips and placed the individual sentences into separate envelopes. One by one, the students volunteered to take an envelope, read the sentence inside silently, and act out the sentence. If a student couldn't read the sentence, I would whisper it to him or her. The other students tried to guess what sentence was presented. This activity was filled with much laughter.

Packing a Suitcase

I drew and cut out pictures of paper suitcases for my students. I asked them to cut and paste onto the suitcases different magazine pictures showing items that they had brought with them on their journey to America. Often the pictures were not available, so instead the students drew these items (such as shirts and rice).

Weekly Evaluation

The closing activity for the week was a short evaluation. I listed the days of the week, along with the activity or activities that we had done during that class period. I asked the students to circle in green those activities that they liked and would like to do again and to circle in red those activities that they didn't like and did not want to do again. I often had samples of each day's work on hand to better illustrate the activities listed on the paper. I collected the survey, reviewed the responses, and acted on the students' comments. If most of the students indicated that they did not like a certain activity, I decided not to offer it again. Sometimes the students offered suggestions on how I could improve the activity.

Later, I reviewed all the work of each student, stapled it together, and gave it back to the students for them to store in their work folders.

Reflections and Student Responses

The video was a very moving experience. My students were in tears. The theme of the story truly represented the interests and experiences of the class. Coming to America, tears, and travel were things that everyone in the class could understand. It provided a good subject for an authentic story. After the students viewed the video, I was concerned that the subject matter was too emotional, but the students were able to write a language experience story.

Even with the use of the video, the photo of the family leaving Thailand and coming to America was equally important to the writing of the story. It framed and clarified the context of the story. It provided more information especially to the students who were able to use only pictures and photos as a channel for information. The story and poem used simple, yet powerful, thoughts and helped focus word-oriented people on the topic of the story.

Extensions

Over time I have used many different pictures that related to the lives and problems of my students as prompts for the authentic stories we wrote as a class. I have used a picture of a family with

37 children, a mother shaking her finger as she scolded her daughter, a man hitting a woman, a man visiting a Chinese medicine store, Edvard Munch's painting of *The Scream*.

After presenting the picture or photo, I routinely asked the following:

1. What do you see?
2. What is the problem?
3. Has this happened to you?
4. How would you solve the problem?

I have added different activities for Choose 3 during the course of our program: One involved counting, classifying, and problem-solving; another, fixing broken equipment; and still another, building a house out of straws. I also found a game similar to "Hangman" to be a popular activity.

— Coming to America II: Born in the USA —

Stella Edwards

Stella created this project influenced by MI Lessons such as Terri Coustan's Coming to America *and Wendy Quiñones's* Homework Students Love.

Subject   Language arts
Curriculum Objective
              To develop students' pride in their cultures and ethnic backgrounds
Time   Students work at home with their families on this assignment and 1 hour/day was given
              for class sharing and/or project making.
Materials Biographies of African American people representing diverse topics from sports to the
              arts; drawing and writing paper with a collection of art and craft supplies, markers, pens,
              tape recorder, and blank tapes

Background

My class consists of mostly African American students between the ages of 19 and 69. Women outnumber men four to one. The average reading grade level is 5.4.

The Lesson

I started with an introduction of several portraits of prominent African Americans such as Paul Laurence Dunbar, Jackie Robinson, Marian Anderson, and Oprah Winfrey. I also got portrait posters on loan to give the students a visual introduction to the author. The books varied in reading levels. I started this exercise by gathering my students in a circle and reading Paul Laurence Dunbar's *Little Brown Baby*.

We then talked about the students' history, and how they came to live in Dayton, Ohio. Many students did not know how their families ended up in Dayton. I then invited them to go home and talk to family members about their family's journey to America and Dayton. It was up to them to select their source and to make up and ask questions. They worked as a group on the types of questions to ask and then chose the questions pertinent to their family members. Many talked to their mothers and grandmothers, and two students interviewed their great-grandmothers. Inspired by Jean Mantzaris's Memory Lane activity, I invited students to bring to class items representing their family history.

The students shared their stories in class through different media. They wrote, drew, shared photographs, recipes, and various artifacts, and one student made a mask to complement their oral stories. This was the first time my students used their own unique smarts to express their history. They talked about what their families endured and were surprised about the similarities in their families' struggles.

The class talked about the value of passing down family stories orally because few grandparents knew how to read, much less write down their family history. Storytelling is an art form that many people around the world have used to sustain their cultures. The students came to this realization after listening to their parents, grandparents, and great-grandparents.

I invited the students to have their elders retell their stories and audiotape them. They really liked this idea, and one young man added drumming to go along with his recording.

We ended the month with a fashion show of ethnic clothes and jewelry. The students hung pictures and craft items on our classroom walls alongside their names. Some volunteered to bring in food to share. In December, the students expanded this lesson by organizing a Kwanzaa celebration.

As a final class project, we expanded on previous writing lessons. Students wrote four to five paragraphs consisting of five sentences each about how they felt when they started this project, their feelings during the interviews with family members, and how they felt afterwards about themselves. The consensus was that they felt pride in themselves individually and as African Americans. As far as I was concerned, the project had met and even exceeded its goal.

Reflections and Student Responses

The students came to see their elders in a new light. Some found a closeness with their grandparents that they didn't have before this assignment. As Catherine put it, "We were too busy to take the time to share and really talk and listen to what they had to say." The students have since shared how important they have become within their own families since they started to "talk stories" with their elders and to record them for future generations to enjoy. Three students wanted to make the journey back "to their roots" in Africa.

The students also came to appreciate each other through this sharing. We talked about other things they shared as members of an African American community, such as music and dance.

— Indoor Gardening —

Terri Coustan

In the following unit, Terri uses the thematic format to develop a series of related lessons. In this case, she encourages her students to draw upon several of their intelligences while working on a gardening unit.

Subject   Language arts and math
Curriculum Objective
        To develop reading, writing, problem-solving, and math (adding and subtracting) skills and learn new vocabulary
Time   Eight sessions (Each activity can stand independently.)

Background

Most of the students in the class are Hmong from the hills of Laos. Some are struggling to communicate orally in English, whereas others have difficulty with reading and writing.

Because my students had been farmers in Laos and China, they brought to this project a great deal of personal experience and interest in gardening. The MI-based instruction introduced in this unit revolves around a gardening theme. I encouraged my students to learn by having them participate in a variety of activities that emphasized different intelligences.

Lesson 1

Planning Home Gardens
Materials   Paper and pencils, garden catalogues

I asked the class to think about the gardens they had had in Laos or China. After a discussion of what they grew and the size of their gardens, the students wrote about them. Some of the students with limited English asked me for words; others drew pictures instead of writing. Each member of the class presented something about a garden from his or her native land.

Following these presentations, I gave each student a seed catalogue. The class worked in groups to review the catalogue and choose the seeds that they would like to order for their home gardens. We listed all the seeds on the blackboard and decided how many packages were to be ordered, along with how much the order would cost. The students had to look very carefully at the catalogue to discover the cost of the individual seed packages. They quickly learned how the catalogue and its individual pages were organized.

The focus of the activities then changed from reading, writing, and drawing to one involving math computation.

Lesson 2

Constructing an Indoor Greenhouse
Materials   Plastic shelving, grow lights, duct tape, plastic sheeting, automatic timer

In preparation for planting their own outdoor gardens, the class decided that they wanted to grow seedlings in school rather than at home because they thought their apartments might be too cold. They chose to assemble ready-made shelving, instead of constructing the shelves from wood, and attached grow lights with duct tape. I gave them the supplies, and they assembled the shelving. The indoor greenhouse was assembled in the kitchen area of our school. Because we had two shelving units, the men assembled one and the women assembled the other. The students were able to assemble the shelves, attach the grow lights with duct tape, and cut the plastic sheeting in long strips after securing it to the shelving, thus allowing for ventilation. I assisted only when called upon.

Preparing Seed Trays
Materials Soil mix, trash bucket, gallon container, long ruler for stirring and leveling the soil, water, seed trays, seeds

The next class session was devoted to preparing the seed trays. I provided compressed soil mix, a bucket, and a gallon container for water. The students mixed the soil with water in a trash bucket. They were able to determine the appropriate amount of water on the basis of their own gardening experience. (Another activity could have been based on the concept of ratios using the ratio of water to soil.)

The students filled the trays with soil and used rulers to level them off. Each student asked for two trays. For seeds, the students had brought in their own dried hot peppers and crushed them, releasing the seeds that they planted. (Our eyes were stinging!) I photographed the activities during the second and third class sessions. These photos played an essential role in the following activity.

Lesson 3

Sequencing Photos and Writing Descriptions
Materials   Photocopies of photographs taken during the past two sessions, paper, paste, pencils

I photocopied selected photographs from the last two activities. I compiled the photos into sets, with enough photos so that each pair of students would receive a complete set. I made certain that the photos I gave them were in random order and then asked the students to work together to sequence the photos in the order that the action had occurred. Deciding on the order of the photos posed some problems, and the students consulted with each other and debated about the order of the photos. After the students had decided on the sequence of the photos, they pasted them on paper and wrote a description for each photo. I assembled the pages and gave the books back to the students.

Creating Timelines
Materials Chart paper, markers

I asked the students to tell me about their lives as farmers in Laos or China.
o   What time do you get up?

o   What do you do next? What did you eat?

o   Who fixed the food?

o   What were the names of the animals?

o   What happened next?

On chart paper, I outlined two hourly schedules for a 24-hour period—one to detail the daily life of a farmer in Laos, the other to show the daily life of a farmer in China. The class shared information about their animals and crops, food, responsibilities of men and women, roles of the children, housing and daily hygiene, the size and distance of their farms from their houses, and the importance of the mountains and rivers in their daily lives. I wrote the information they shared on the appropriate charts. The two schedules provided an opportunity for the students to compare and contrast their lives in their native lands. A good class discussion followed.

Illustrating an Hour in the Life of a Farmer
Materials Timelines showing daily schedules, markers, heavy construction paper, drawing materials, writing materials

I asked each student to select one hour from one of the daily schedules to illustrate, first through a drawing and then through a story. Some of the students asked to take their work home and recruited the help of their children. The stories included information about village life. I matted each picture onto black poster paper along with the story. I posted the work on the bulletin board after they had presented it to the class.

Lesson 4

Making a Model Garden

Materials Blocks of $1/2$-inch thick Styrofoam™ purchased from a craft store, cut into 12- by 12-inch sections; metal coat hangers; Popsicle® sticks; garden catalogues; glue; scissors; fishing line

We discussed what each student would like to grow in his or her own garden. After our discussion, I gave each student a block of green 12- by 12-inch Styrofoam™, Popsicle® sticks, scissors, glue, and a garden catalogue. I asked the students to cut out pictures of the vegetables or flowers that they would like to grow in their garden. The students attached the pictures to the sticks with glue and then placed the sticks in the foam in any order that pleased them. Some of the students wrote the names of the plants on the pictures; others numbered the plants and provided a key to the placement of the plants in the garden.

When the project was completed, I slipped each model garden through a metal coat hanger, keeping the curved part on top. I then used tape to attach the bottom of the hangers to the underside of the foam. Using fishing line, I hung the gardens from the ceiling. The students were very surprised to see their gardens hanging when they arrived in class the following day.

Playing the Vegetable "Wheel of Fortune®" Game

Materials Large pieces of poster paper; metal fastener; handmade cardboard arrow; pictures of vegetables; play money; clear, sticky shelf covering; index cards

I taped several pieces of poster board together to form a rectangle approximately 48 by 52 inches. I drew a large circle and divided it into sections. On some of the sections, I pasted vegetable pictures; on other sections, I wrote different amounts of money, preceded by either the word *Win* or *Lose*. I covered the entire poster with clear, sticky shelving paper so that the arrow could move smoothly. Finally, I attached an arrow to the middle of the wheel by securing it with a metal fastener and tape.

Then using index cards, I made about 30 game cards. The text on each card involved garden problems or successes. For a success, the students would win money; for a problem, the students would lose money. For example, one card might read, "You forgot to water the garden, and the tomatoes died. Lose $10." Alternatively, another might read, "Your corn is ripe and ready to eat. Collect $15." I tried to provide enough cards so that each of the 20 students would have three or four turns.

The rules of the game were easy. First, I selected a treasurer or banker to handle the money. Then I gave each student $100 of play money in an envelope. When the game began, each student came up to spin the arrow. If the arrow landed on the vegetable picture, the student drew an index card and read the card. If the arrow landed on a dollar amount, the student either won or lost the amount indicated. The banker handled all of the transactions.

The game got very spirited as the students ran out of money and had to solve this problem. My students borrowed from each other. The game involved a lot of computational skills, as well as reading and vocabulary. At the end of the game, the student with the most money left was declared the winner.

Reflections and Student Responses

The students enjoyed sharing information about their native lands and comparing and contrasting their farming experiences with classmates from different cultures. Everyone was able to participate in the Vegetable "Wheel of Fortune®" game. The children had a great time. The adults had fun adding and subtracting their money.

When I took the time to mat pictures or mount them on colored cardboard and post them in class, I found that the students paid more attention to them. Maybe it is because I had shown my appreciation for their work by making an extra effort to display it.

Extensions

o   Making a Vegetable Bingo game is another activity that would fit well in this unit. The students could construct their own bingo boards.

o   The class could hold a vegetable sale with the vegetables that were grown in the indoor garden. The students could price the plants, publicize the sale, and decide how to spend the profits.

— A Trip to the Clinic —

Diane Paxton

In this lesson, Diane shows how she built upon her students' goals to improve their communication skills in health care settings.

Subject   Language arts
Curriculum Objective
              To develop reading and writing skills, and health-care-related vocabulary
Time   4 to 6 hours

Background

The class is a beginning level ESOL class, and the students all have in common a low level of literacy in their first language. We use both Spanish and English in this class. The students had told me that they wanted to learn words to use at the health clinic.

The Lesson

Review Health Vocabulary
Materials Commercial ESOL text, strips of colored paper

The first activities that the students worked on introduced and reinforced vocabulary related to health. From a commercial ESOL text containing vocabulary and corresponding illustrations, the students learned words that they might need when visiting a doctor's office. They worked on a picture dictionary activity where they matched up drawings with health-related vocabulary words that had been written on separate strips of colored paper. From a list we had developed together, the students practiced pronouncing medical terms containing the Spanish/English cognates "-cion" and "-tion," emphasizing rhythmic patterns as they went along. As a group, we devised a visual and written strategy for remembering syllabic emphasis by which the students learned to underline the strongest syllable in each word. They also enjoyed reviewing their newly acquired health vocabulary words by playing "Simon Says."

Board Game
Materials Poster board, colored paper, colored markers, glue, scissors, copies of clinic-related drawings from a commercial text, index cards, playing pieces, dice

I created this game to give my students an active way to reinforce what we had studied in class and to practice specific language skills that they told me they needed whenever they visited the health clinic.

The process of designing and making this game took about 4 hours. As I worked on it at home, I considered the various attributes of a board game that I wanted to include and the language I hoped the students would practice when they played it. I also considered what they had told me about the spatial arrangement of the health clinic and their concerns about managing in that environment.

First, I taped two pieces of poster board together to create a large playing area. Then I made the signs to designate the various "rooms" that the students would "visit" in the clinic (Waiting Room, Admissions, Blood Pressure Room, Emergency Room, and Specialist Doctor Room). I arranged the rooms on the board and sketched a winding path between them.

Using vocabulary the students had already worked on in class and other words that might be associated with that room, I wrote cards to correspond with the various rooms. In an attempt to deemphasize the linguistic intelligence (reading and writing), I tried to write cards that encouraged tasks related to all the intelligences. For example, some of the Waiting Room's cards read, "You are bored. Sing a song." "What time is it?" and "You need exercise. Dance with a friend." I added to the board copies of the drawings used earlier during the picture dictionary activity. Then I cut out and placed colored-paper squares on the board to create the winding path.

To put drama into the game, I made additional cards that sent the players backwards and forwards to different rooms. "You have a stomach ache. Go to the Specialist Doctor Room," "Emergency! Go to the Blood Pressure Room," and "You forgot your blue insurance card. Go back home." I also added the Hospital, to which players were sent by only a few cards in the Emergency and Specialist Room stacks. Once in the Hospital, the player had to miss a turn and then start again at home.

To keep players busy between turns, I also created cards that asked the players to fill in different types of forms for admissions and prescription information. Then I made up small forms listing questions regarding their medical histories.

To encourage vocabulary practice, I found playing pieces that represent items from daily life: lock, bird, button, candle, strawberry, leaf, matches, and electrical plug.

Reflections and Student Responses

After we finished playing the game, we assessed how useful the activity had been by talking about what the students had learned and those areas of language use that they had practiced. We listed these on the board. The students offered the following responses:

o   Practice with numbers

o   Learning and playing at the same time

o   Reading and writing

o   Talking

o   Learning what to say when you go to the doctor

o   Practice how to fill out appointment cards and forms

o   Names of colors and playing pieces

o   Names of places in the clinic

o   How to say a medical problem in English

o   Nutrition: Eat more vegetables and less fat

o   Remember to exercise (dancing is exercise)

o   Practice what you say at an appointment

o   How to say the time

o   Talking in English can be fun

An important result of this game was that, after generating this more formal assessment list, the students began to speak enthusiastically about using aloe and other herbal remedies; playing the game invited discussion of their traditional methods for family health maintenance. Each student knew a recipe for healing anything from diabetes to hair loss to infected feet.

Extensions

o   A game about thinking about what kind of job or career you want.

o   A game about job hunting, interviewing, and work issues.

o   A game about getting to know a new neighborhood, city, or country.

o   A game about nutrition and health, family issues, housing, or transportation issues.

o   A game related to GED preparation in content areas or as practice for the citizenship examination.

o   Have the students themselves design and make games related to their themes of study, life issues, or experiences! (See "Jobopoly," created by Jean Mantzaris, later in this chapter.)

— Natural Medicines Book —

Diane Paxton

In this lesson Diane builds on her students' knowledge about natural remedies.

Subject   Language arts
Curriculum Objective
            To develop writing skills
Time   16 hours

Background

The students in this class were elderly, beginning level ESOL students. Our work on this natural medicines book grew out of the students' interest in and their knowledge about home remedies. I had been looking for a high-interest topic from which to further develop their literacy skills in a writing workshop format. This was the third book we made together, so they were familiar with the idea of creating a book in English class. However, the process for writing each book was different and progressively gave more literacy practice and responsibility over to the students. The following lesson grew directly out of the previous lesson where we had played a board game and assessed its usefulness as a tool for learning English.

I have listed here the writing, grammar, and editing activities we did while writing the book, but it is important to understand that this work was done in a workshop format and tasks overlapped.

The Lesson

Sharing Favorite Recipes

Once we decided to make a book, the students shared their favorite natural recipes. Because they were so interesting, we decided to include personal stories about where each recipe came from or a particular person whom the recipe had helped. I suggested that we take step-by-step photographs as they created their recipes, and, after that, the students organized who would bring what utensils and ingredients for the photo sessions.

Setting their own pace for writing their recipes in the two languages, students worked individually and in pairs. We discussed strategies for writing, editing techniques, grammar, and vocabulary, both with individual students and with the whole class.

We talked about the ingredients and utensils that they needed to make the recipes and made drawings of those items, labeling them in English for practice and reference. We gathered ingredients, made the recipes in the kitchen of the community center, and photographed the students during each step of the creation of their recipes. The students worked either alone or with a classmate.

Sequencing Photos

Following this, I gave each student his or her photos in a jumbled pile and had the students sequence the photos in the correct order. Working with another classmate, the students had to talk through the process of making the recipe. This helped the students to begin articulating the steps and amounts needed so that, when they started to write down the recipe, this information would be clearer.

Writing the Recipes

We discussed ways to write the recipes down clearly, so that a person could read them and know how to make them without having the author present to answer questions. We looked at recipe books for examples. They decided to make the book bilingual so that it would be useful to a greater number of people.

After we began the process of writing down the recipes, it became evident that the students needed to be able to access more vocabulary words, especially verbs. I made up a grammar handout with actual sentences taken from the recipes they were writing. We practiced from the handout and did a cloze fill-in-the-blanks activity, using appropriate verbs to complete the given sentences.

Later, I used the same sentences, written on strips of paper, chopped into individual words and stored in separate envelopes, for the students to reassemble in sentence form. I had made two levels so that they could try the less complicated sentence structures first.

They continued to write and edit the recipes in Spanish and English. I encouraged the students to try various techniques, such as

o   peer editing.

o   scribing by the more advanced students for students with limited writing ability.

o   sharing writing, dictionary, and vocabulary strategies.

Using a Language Experience Approach process, we wrote the introduction together. The students told me what they wanted to say, and I scribed it for them on the board. We reorganized, translated, and corrected our work together so that it expressed the students' feelings and ideas.

Illustrating the Book

Finally, they drew pictures of the ingredients, along with illustrations of other trees, fruits, and flowers from their native countries. We decided to use one of their drawings for the cover, so they voted for both the cover picture and the title.

Speaking Practice

We read the individual recipes aloud many times throughout this process so that they could practice pronunciation.

We had the book printed and bound at a local copy center with funds from the education budget. In the end, for pronunciation practice, the students read the entire book aloud again.

Reflections and Student Responses

Their work on this book gave these students a greater acceptance of nontraditional activities in the classroom, in addition to explicit realizations that the class had affected their lives in broader, deeper ways. From comments that they made as we read from their finished book of natural medicines, I saw that they had developed stronger connections to the written word, both in their own language and in English. This was because, for the first time, they saw that writing could come from them personally and literacy could reflect their experiences, the knowledge they had shared in their communities, and their individual voices.

When I asked students about the process of writing the book, they focused on how important it had been to them personally, as the following quotes highlight:

> This is a source of pride for us. I took the other books we made to El Salvador and showed them to my children. Jesus and I get two copies because we are two, so I leave one in my country with them and keep one here for us. I told them that this is the work we do with our teacher. They read them. We read them together.

> My daughter looks at these books like literature. She reads them at home and studies them. This book is like literature for us; we feel proud of it.

> Every book we make is better. The first ones were good, and this one is even better. We have other teachers, but no one makes books with us like this. This is our literature.

Final Assessment of the Health Unit

At the end of the whole unit, I made a large chart with visual reminders of all the things we had done that connected to health. (I thank Terri Coustan for this assessment idea.) I drew a picture to represent the game and the camera, and I used actual grammar handouts and pages of their written drafts. These were written across the top of the paper. The students' names were written down the side. Pointing to and reminding them of the various activities, I asked the students what they thought had helped them learn English the most. I was gratified to hear that four students out of six said that everything we had done in class had helped them to learn.

One student's comments from this assessment indicate how comfortable the students had become at expressing their learning preferences.

> Photos of the recipes are good because it's a memory for the next day when we write. Playing the game helped a little bit because you put your mind in the game. The grammar is good because these [recipe nouns and verbs] are things that we use every day. It's useful.

— Heroin and Heroes: Miniprojects —

Meg Costanzo

Meg found the following MI-inspired "mini-unit" format successful with her multi-level class that met for only a few hours a week.

> I use the "I Can" exercise when we study verbs. Then we do the Diamante Poem as a review of nouns, verbs, and adjectives. It has always been a huge success. Today I did it with my class, and Ivory, a 70-year-old man who is a pastor and the founder of a school for the disadvantaged, loved doing. He said he wants to show the teachers at his school so they can do it with the young students there.
>
> ~ Helen Sablan, AMI Sourcebook Pilot Teacher

Subject   Health
Curriculum Objective
            To develop writing, research, and critical thinking skills
Time   3 to 6 hours
Materials Newspaper or magazine articles dealing with information regarding drugs and drug abuse; lined and drawing paper; pens, pencils, and markers

Background

I frequently brought into class newspaper and magazine articles that I felt would be of interest to my GED students. Following my example, some of the students began to do the same. Very often, those selections became the focus of "mini-units," activities that stemmed from the topics discussed in the articles.

This unit plan evolved from a class discussion centering on an article on heroin abuse that had appeared in our local newspaper. The student who brought in this article was outraged at the idea that the paper would print an accompanying color picture that showed a middle-aged couple, sitting in the living room, injecting themselves with this drug. She felt that this graphic picture was inappropriate for a newspaper that was accessible to many children. I asked her what she thought we should do in response to this article. The student replied that she thought that we should write a letter of complaint to the editor.

The class's interest in the subject was so intense that I decided to create a "mini-unit" around the theme of drug abuse.

Lessons 1 to 3

The Drug Abuse Mini-Unit

Getting Started

After reading this article about the increased use of heroin in our area, the students brainstormed a list of questions about this drug. Then we read an encyclopedia article on heroin and searched for the answers to our questions.

Research

Some questions remained, so I taught the students how to do research on the Internet. They evaluated various web sites to determine how helpful they would be in providing information on the topic.

Choose One: Drug Abuse Mini-Unit

I then gave the class a list of activities related to our study of drug abuse. After going over each one and discussing the type of work each entailed, I asked the students which activities they were drawn to and which ones they had no interest in. We talked about how their preferences related to their strongest intelligences. Finally, I gave the class 2 weeks to complete the following assignment.

Select one of the following activities to complete by _____. You may work alone or in small groups.

1. Think about a song that deals with drug use. What message is the singer trying to get across to his or her audience? How do the lyrics and musical arrangement help to convey that message? How does the song make you feel?

2. Write a short skit that centers on what someone could do to help a friend who is abusing drugs. Include at least two characters. Present the skit to the class.

3. Write a letter to the editor of the *Rutland Herald* expressing your opinion of the article and its accompanying photograph, entitled "Heroin Addicts Risk All for Drug That Rules Them."

4. Some people feel that the drug problem in this country could be eliminated if drugs were made legal.

   a. Survey at least 20 people, asking them their opinions on legalizing drugs. Design a way to collect your data. Chart and graph your results. Or

   b. Write an essay expressing your opinion on this issue.

5. Draw a political cartoon that expresses your feelings about drug abuse. Include a caption that explains your drawing.

6. Make a chart that lists the various types of drugs and information about them. Organize your information under several headings.

7. Plan your own activity that addresses the issue of drug abuse. Write up a proposal describing what you want to do, and present it to me at our next class.

Reflections and Student Responses

The students reported enjoying this type of mini-unit. One student told me,

> I like the class projects. Everyone gets to participate. You have choices. You feel more comfortable when you have choice. Then you're willing to do more and you do better.

It is interesting to note that I found a strong, positive correlation between the students' preferred intelligences and the activities to which they reported being drawn. Many chose to take one of the choices I had presented and modify it to suit their own interests and talents. For instance, one student sketched a drawing and expanded it into a cartoon strip that told the story of the excuses given by a person using drugs to delude himself into thinking that he doesn't have a drug problem. When I looked back at the two activities this student had earlier indicated as his preferences, I noted that he had listed the skit and the cartoon; he found a creative way to combine the two into one product that synthesized his two interests.

One student said he felt uncomfortable discussing the topic of drug abuse. I accommodated him and gave him another assignment.

Lesson 4

People We Admire Mini-Unit

Essay Writing

The following is another example of a writing assignment and mini-unit that I wrote in response to interest in a current events topic.

Think of some public figure, either living or deceased, whom you admire. Write an essay of about 200 words telling something about this person and explaining why you think so highly of him or her.

Choose One: People We Admire Mini-Unit

You have just finished writing an essay about a person whom you greatly admire. Now choose one of the activities listed below to complete by _____. If you wish, you can think of your own activity to do instead of selecting one from the list. Then write a short proposal outlining what you plan to do, and discuss it with me before you begin your work.

1. If you were making a movie about this person, what type of music would you play in the background? Be prepared to discuss the reasons for your selection(s).

2. Write a song about this person.

3. Design a set of commemorative stamps that depict four important aspects about this person's life.

4. Write an imaginary interview between you and this person or actually interview the person.

5. Create a timeline chronicling the significant events in this person's life.

6. Write a poem about this person. You might want to use the format of a diamante poem (Figure 4.4).

7. Reflect upon the reasons that others might admire you. Complete a diamante poem about yourself. Share what the experience of writing this poem was like. You also may choose to share the poem with the rest of the class.

8. Choreograph a dance or present a skit that tells something about this person's life.

9. Make up a trivia quiz that highlights at least 10 important events in this person's life. Try starting with easy questions, and then work up to ones that are more difficult.

10. Design a facts page or résumé that outlines important information about this person.

Figure 4.4. Format for a Diamante Poem

			First Name			
		Adjective		Adjective		
	Verb		Verb		Verb	
Noun		Noun		Noun		Noun
[Write a Sentence About the Person for This Line.]						
Noun		Noun		Noun		Noun
	Verb		Verb		Verb	
		Adjective		Adjective		
			Last Name			

Sample Diamante Poem

			Sally			
		bright		diligent		
	reads		questions		attends	
novels		magazines		authority		classes
Sally is a bright diligent student and a caring mother.						
mother		daughter		student		wife
	works		manages		cares	
		ambitious		caring		
			Smith			

— "Jobopoly" —

Jean Mantzaris

Jean developed the following lesson to help acquaint her students with the types of jobs they are likely to find available in their community and to educate them about the various requirements needed for each job.

Subject   Career counseling
Curriculum Objective
         To learn about careers and their education and training requirements based on student interest
Time   2^1/$_2$ hours (45 minutes to design the game, 45 minutes for a trial run, and another hour to actually play the game)
Materials   Poster paper, about twenty 11- by 14-inch pieces; magic markers; dice; play money; index cards

Background

I developed this lesson to help my ABE/GED students explore their interests and needs in light of the types of higher education and training necessary for various career choices. Before this activity, the students learned about MI theory and had assessed their own intelligences. They also learned about the Connecticut School-to-Career Clusters. Through class discussions, the students reflected upon the relationship between their own intelligences and those intelligences required for jobs in the various career clusters. The clusters include Arts and Media; Business and Finance; Construction: Technologies and Design; Environmental, Natural Resources, and Agriculture; Government; Education and Human Services; Health and Biosciences; Retail, Tourism, Recreation, and Entrepreneurship; Technologies: Manufacturing, Communication, and Repair.

The Lesson

Introduction

I told the students that they were going to use their knowledge of the eight Connecticut School-to-Career Clusters to design a Monopoly-style game that would help them learn more about how to prepare for the various jobs that are available in our state. I shared with the class an idea about playing large-scale games where the players acted as the game pieces on a giant game board that was placed on the floor. The students agreed to this plan.

Designing "Jobopoly"

I told the students that it was their job to design the game board and set the rules for play. They came up with the following ideas:

o   A series of 11- by 14-inch paper rectangles to form the perimeter of a 10- by 14-foot game board, with four openings to serve as "Entry Points."

o   Eight 9-inch diameter circles cut from poster board, each one labeled with the name of one of the clusters and placed on the center of the board.

o   Twenty "Chance" cards.

The rectangles had the following labels: "High School Diploma" (2 spaces), "Four-Year College" (2 spaces), "Internship/Apprenticeship" (2 spaces), "Community College" (2 spaces), "Graduate School" (1 space), "Pass Go, Collect $500" (1 space), "Chance" (1 space), and "Go to Jail" (1 space). [The "High School Diploma" spaces were free, but most of the other spaces had a cost attached to them.

The "Chance" cards listed good and bad events that might influence the players' ability to meet their career goals. For example, "You win the lottery and have enough money to attend 4 years of college," or "You have to pay for child care for your two children," or "Your application for federal aid has been approved."

Playing the Game

Before they began to play, the students thought about their strongest intelligences, decided which career cluster they wanted to enter, and determined the requirements for the "job" that they wanted to pursue. All the players started at "Go" with $500 and moved around the board as their turns came up. They purchased or won by "Chance" the necessary requirements to enter their chosen center circle. They could purchase a requirement only if they had landed on the appropriate space, and they needed to collect the requirements in the correct order. For example, they could not purchase a diploma from "Community College" or enter into an "Internship/ Apprenticeship" until they had landed on "High School Diploma." Once the students had accumulated all the necessary requirements, they needed to land on an "Entry Point" in order to move onto a circle in the center. The first student to achieve his or her career goal was deemed the winner.

Reflections and Student Responses

It is important to give the game a trial run before you play. This gives the students an opportunity to work out any problems that might arise and is a great problem-solving exercise in itself. For instance, when the students tried the game, they realized that one space for "High School Diploma" would have been adequate. They could then decide how to adjust the board to suit their findings.

When given the opportunity to solve this problem (how to go about preparing for a career) and create this product ("Jobopoly" game), my students were enthusiastic and cooperative. They were capable of matching the aspects of various careers to the different intelligences and helped each other in deciding the requirements necessary for various career choices. This activity proved to be a great opportunity for me to acquaint my students with local higher education opportunities, available federal financial aid, and local job opportunities. One student commented,

> I always thought a career was for someone else. Now I see I can really be a youth officer. Even the thought makes me proud.

Chapter 5: STUDENT RESPONSES TO MI PRACTICES: THE AMI EXPERIENCE

Introduction

How did AMI students respond to MI-informed practices?

> My creativity has been dormant for so long that to exercise it a little makes me long to use it more and more.
>
> ~ Adult Secondary level student of Wendy Quiñones, AMI Teacher–Researcher

> I think the MI activities are really educational and fun. A lot of people that I know would love MI. I like MI because it tells you a lot about yourself and who you really are.
>
> ~ GED student of Helen Sablan, AMI Sourcebook Pilot Teacher

> [MI activities] cause you to open up your mind without even realizing it. . . everyone has different strengths. If we all put our minds together, we can figure out any problem. I am learning more stuff in this little class than in most high school classes.
>
> ~ GED student of Helen Sablan, AMI Sourcebook Pilot Teacher

> I think that we as adults know where our strengths and weaknesses are. I feel that I know I am not strong at math, but I know a little bit, and I also feel I am strong at dealing with people. I don't know, I guess I don't like who I am to be labeled.
>
> ~ Math student of Jan Tucker, AMI Sourcebook Pilot Teacher

> I prefer hands-on because it clarifies everything. If it was all workbook, I wouldn't do well 'cause I'd lose my interest. I wouldn't stay long. . .
>
> ~ GED student of Martha Jean, AMI Teacher–Researcher

> "I don't like when we do that stuff," he said, gesturing to the collages on the wall, "It's for children." Two months later, "Everything in this class helps us. . . . I like the class a lot, and the group work too."
>
> ~ Intermediate level ESOL student of Diane Paxton, AMI Teacher–Researcher

"How did your students respond?" is often the first and most frequently asked question posed to a teacher trying something new in her classroom. Rightly, teachers put great store in how students react to and evaluate the teaching and learning experiences they are offered. By the same token, being mindful of and responsive to students' reactions is a basic ingredient to good MI-informed practices.

With that in mind, we devote this chapter to sharing the insights the AMI Study codirectors gained in the AMI Study by looking closely at students' responses to the MI experiences in which they participated. As the quotes above suggest, students' reactions were diverse, ranging from resistant to enthusiastic. We have found two variables particularly germane to explaining and anticipating student response: the type of MI practice (MI Reflections or MI-informed Instruction) and the students' instructional context (ABE, GED/Adult

Diploma, ESOL). In this chapter, we look at student responses from these two vantage points.

How Students Responded to MI Reflections (MIR)

As described in Chapter 2, MIR activities are meant to teach students about MI theory and to use the theory for self-understanding. MI Reflections can occur in a number of different ways, in the form of self-assessment surveys, reflection journals, and hands-on activities. Of the ten AMI teacher researchers, nine conducted some form of MIR activities with their students. The extent to which they undertook these activities varied. Some teachers chose only to introduce MI theory, others facilitated occasional reflection activities, and others maintained MIR as a regular part of the class. For each of the teachers, whether and how MI Reflection activities continued to unfold in her classroom were intrinsically related to her students' reactions.

In virtually every group of AMI learners whose teachers decided to introduce MI theory, there were students who reacted positively from the beginning, appreciating the idea that each of us is smart in our own way and that our diverse abilities should be valued and put to good use inside and outside of the classroom. Many adults saw MI theory's relevance to their lives outside of school as workers and parents. When prompted by their teachers, they began to relate their MI Reflections to possible careers.

After implementing a variety of MIR activities throughout her GED course, AMI teacher Meg Costanzo concluded, "Students appreciate having their intelligences acknowledged and valued. Many have never had the opportunity to claim their intelligences before this experience" (Kallenbach & Viens, 2001, p. 36). This is what one of her students wrote after doing the AMI self-assessment Meg developed:

> This survey actually helped me think about what I wanted to do. When I originally did my High School (alternative) diploma, I had no idea what I wanted to do, or that I was good at working with people. Now I'm thinking of going into social work. (Costanzo, 1997a)

Reflecting on one's intelligence strengths proved very fruitful for career exploration. Guidance counselor Jean Mantzaris received an overwhelmingly positive response from the 11 students who participated in her 12-week MI-based career-counseling course. She began by teaching her students about MI theory and by having them assess their own intelligences. (See AMI Survey: "How You Are Smart?") Both Jean and her students found the MI self-assessments to complement more traditional career aptitude tests. Jean was pleasantly surprised that her students were very motivated to try the new approaches to guidance counseling. Jean reports,

> My students were very willing to try out childhood games and activities without dismissing these activities as silly … to connect the way "they were" to the way "they are" and relate these strengths to possible careers.… This activity really put the "me" into the process. It provided a significant addition to our program that already includes [several] other career decision-making activities. (Mantzaris, 1998)

Some students began to see MI theory's potential to change the way their children were being educated. AMI teacher Bonnie Fortini's students related the message of MI theory not to their own childhoods but to what they hoped for their children. One father-to-be said he would use his knowledge of MI to make sure no one ever made his child feel stupid the way he felt in school. Two of his classmates wrote that they were more willing to try to learn after learning about MI theory. One woman said that through learning about MI, she learned that it was ok to be different, and that MI was a different way to look at herself.

Other students gradually warmed to MI Reflections, recognizing their relevance only after engaging in related activities over time. For example, Meg's student Roland began with a healthy dose of skepticism about what MI theory had to offer him. Early in the program, Roland commented, "What good is being intelligent [spatially]? I might as well stick to woodworking." Meg writes,

> Roland's acceptance of his strongest intelligence and his willingness to apply it to the writ-

ing process developed over the course of the semester. In January he could not "find himself" in the descriptions of any of the intelligences. By May, he was claiming his intelligence without my prompting, but still not drawing upon it voluntarily when faced with the challenge of a writing assignment.... By June, Roland had recognized that a web was an effective way for him to gather his ideas before attempting to write an essay. (Kallenbach & Viens, 2001, p. 38)

Some students did not connect with MI theory at all or see the value in thinking and talking about "intelligences." To Debbie, one of Betsy Cornwell's students, MI was "a lot of big words I don't understand." Even when Betsy simplified the MI language to "word smart," "body smart," and so on, she felt this had little effect on her students' attitudes about MI theory. With Debbie, in particular, the issue was not simply the vocabulary but rather her concept of what it means to be smart: "'Cause if they was a smart learner they would not be asking for help. You'd already know all the answers. If they were smart they would not need school, and they would not need teachers" (Kallenbach & Viens, 2001, p. 20). Betsy's next step was to try to examine with Debbie her view of smart people and, by extension, of herself. As long as Debbie felt smart people never asked for help or needed teachers, she could not possibly feel smart in any intelligence while being a student.

Some students' objections and unwillingness to engage in MI Reflections seemed to be more rooted in unfamiliarity and lack of experience with metacognitive practices, that is, thinking about their learning. They didn't necessarily come in with a firm position against MI Reflections, but rather this practice was new to them.

Student Responses to MI-informed Instruction

MI-informed lessons are the result of planning content using the eight intelligences and the major tenets of MI theory as a framework (see Chapters 1 and 3). Teachers inform their instruction with MI theory to build in opportunities for students to use different intelligences in the course of learning English, learning to read, or preparing for the GED. A

range of activities and instructional strategies are included within this family of MI applications, including more hands-on activities around a particular topic; using a project-based approach; and giving students options in how they process information and demonstrate understanding.

All 10 AMI teachers carried out some form of MI-based instruction. Whereas two teachers chose to implement only a few MI-based activities, most alternated equally between MI and what could be called more traditional lessons. For a few teachers, an MI-informed approach to lessons was very similar to their previous practices, serving to enhance and extend the work they were already doing.

Overall, most students in the AMI classes came to view MI-based learning activities in a positive light. As with MI Reflections, some people took time to shift their perceptions, whereas others embraced the more nontraditional activities from the beginning. For example, Martha Jean's GED-prep students responded enthusiastically from the start. In their weekly end-of-class group reflections, students repeatedly shared with Martha their view that MI-informed approaches kept them engaged and learning. As Martha writes, this engagement translated into improved attendance and attention in class:

> After several years of seeing these [LD and ADD] students consistently struggle with workbooks and then quickly depart, or attending class but not doing their work, it was an amazing discovery that something seemed to be motivating them to stay with the class, attend full sessions, and/or complete the work. Monthly and total hours of attendance increased in my MI-informed class.... The only thing I had changed was the once-weekly addition of an MI-informed lesson. (Kallenbach & Viens, 2001, p. 115)

Like her colleagues, Martha used her students' responses to help plan MI-based instruction. For example, her MI-based classroom activity ended with reflections on how it had helped students with that particular GED content area, like editorial cartoons, proportions, or planets. Her students noted that the Choose 3: Proportions had been helpful, but they found "planets" too broad a topic. As a result, Martha decided to narrow the scope of future Choose 3 activities where students chose from among eight or so learning activities roughly corresponding to the eight intelligences.

Bonnie Fortini's students mentioned as their favorite a math activity with candy "because you could see and feel and eat it." Another favorite was an activity about fractions using magazine cutouts. However, this time it was not the medium but rather the mode that the students seemed to value the most: "It was much more fun this time because we worked as a team." And, "The activity on the fractions was fun and I learned from it. I also worked with a classmate, which helped me learn easier." Students in virtually every AMI classroom echoed Bonnie's students' praise for group work. Where students had not had many opportunities to work with their peers previously, the teachers were surprised by the positive impact of the group-learning mode. One of Meg Costanzo's students commented, "Math is a subject that doesn't come too easily for me. If I do it in a group, someone else might have an easier way of doing the problem to help me out. Drawing the pictures out tonight really helped me with perimeter and area" (Costanzo, 1997a).

MI-informed instruction probably did not match most students' notions of an ESOL, ABE, or GED class. Their past educational experiences probably led them to expect a more traditionally run classroom. Although many students appreciated entertaining or playful learning activities, others were suspicious, at least initially, of activities that seemed to offer too much fun. Several students balked at MI-based activities as being childish. Perhaps some students felt that the curriculum was being "dumbed down" for them. Yet other students may have found the more traditional paper-and-pencil–based approaches a better fit with their learning preferences.

Many students started with negative or at least hesitant reactions to MI-informed activities, but they came to embrace them relatively quickly. This was true whether or not they were aware of the connection to MI. It was often the teachers' persistence with the activities in spite of the students'

ambivalent, sometimes even hostile, response that broke the ice. For example, Diane Paxton's elderly ESOL students seemed to shift from a distinctly "traditional" perspective on effective English instruction to enthusiasm for MI-based activities. One woman who had criticized a drama project as "juvenile" in the beginning of the semester was full of praise later in the semester for MI-informed activities. She later commented about the *Natural Medicines* book project, "My daughter looks at these books like literature. She reads them at home and studies them" (Kallenbach & Viens, 2001, p. 167).

Dianne Marlowe writes about one particularly resistant student, John, who ultimately described the MI-informed lessons in which he participated as "awesome." He passed his GED and, as Dianne notes, "He really did a great job on the projects. He says that he will never forget how to figure areas and feels he could actually teach someone else to make a quilt. He said he is proud of his work and that he will never forget this class" (Marlowe, 1997). Another male member of the class wrote,

> At the beginning of this whole quilt thing I was totally against it. But with application and a little push, it didn't seem so bad. I thought that only women did quilts, but as I remember from a child, the football player Rosie Greer used to make quilts so that made me all right with making quilts. Once I finished I thought it was over, but it wasn't. We all got together and joined in. We put our heart, soul, and mind into this quilt and I could say once again that I was proud to participate. (p. 10)

Time and experience with MI-based activities seemed to get students who were initially uncomfortable with such activities to accept, and often prefer, MI-based activities as a significant (but not exclusive) part of the instruction. One of Meg Costanzo's students concluded,

> I like the class projects. Everyone gets to participate. You have choices. You feel more comfortable when you have choice. Then you're willing to do more and you do better. (Kallenbach & Viens, 2001, p. 48)

Student Responses "In Context"

The AMI experience indicates that both ABE and ESOL students who are at a low literacy level have a distinct lack of interest in MIR activities. Our hunch is that they see little relevance in MI to themselves and their learning. Like Betsy's student Debbie, they may have difficulty relating to the idea of being smart in any way. Or they may view self-reflection as self-indulgent. They have not had opportunities to develop the metacognitive skills that are brought to bear in MIR activities.

ESOL instructors Terri Coustan and Diane Paxton both met with student disinterest when they introduced MI Reflections. Neither teacher found it useful or necessary to have students talk about MI theory or their own intelligences in order to implement MI-based lessons. Terri also had a major language barrier with her students, which complicated how she could articulate the ideas of MI theory to her students. This made it nearly impossible to know whether students understood MI theory or its connection to themselves and their curriculum.

GED-level students tended to respond more positively to MIR activities, although there were exceptions. However, at the GED level, resistance can form if the connection between the MI-based activities and the students' goals is not clear to the students. GED and diploma preparation students, in particular, are driven by the goal of getting a high school credential, usually as fast as possible. They rightfully ask, "What do these MI activities have to do with passing the GED test?" Ensuring a "tight fit" between students' primary goals and MI-based instruction, and making that connection clear to students, helps students understand and accept MI-informed approaches, particularly when the activities are new to the class. For example, Martha Jean's Choose 3 lessons directly addressed content on the GED tests. The AMI teachers found that yoking MI-based activities to MI Reflections worked quite well to dissolve student resistance to MI-based activities. Through reflection, students were able to see the relationship between the MI activities and their ability to reach their goals.

At the same time, Martha Jean and Meg Costanzo found that as their GED students approached test readiness, they needed to transition from a more diverse, MI-informed approach to a more narrow strategy of test preparation. These students wanted and needed practice with specific test materials and test-taking skills. They allowed these students to limit their participation in their MI-based curriculum so they could focus on taking practice tests.

Conclusion

Student response is the litmus test for if and how teachers use MI-informed practices. By tracking their students' reactions, teachers can gauge whether particular approaches or activities are effective with their students. Student response helps teachers determine how to proceed with MI practices and how particular activities should be revised to meet students' goals and to help students understand the MI-learning goal connection. We saw that students who came to embrace MI typically did so because of engaging in MIR activities in combination with MI-based lessons.

For many students, participation in the AMI Study with their teachers meant moving into unfamiliar educational territory, particularly reflection: reflecting on their intelligence strengths, thinking about what learning strategies and activities help them learn, and having discussions about learning. Several AMI teachers noted that the introduction of MI practices correlated with increases in student initiative, control, and student "voice" (see Chapter 3). That is, students were more able and willing to express their opinions. In that spirit, we end this chapter with advice from Meg Costanzo's students to teachers in order to help them plan effective lessons for adult learners:

o   Take the time to get to know your students.

o   Listen to the student's needs.

o   Students have to know their goals.

o   [The MI] profile will help you know which way to teach. Look for similarities in profiles and use that approach.

o   Try to figure out why students don't understand something and then use a different approach, not just the same thing over and over again.

o   Use more "hands-on" activities and different learning tools.

o   Use creative ways to get the students involved. They make learning fun and interesting. MI theory can help because it leads to creativity in lesson planning.

o   Get everyone to participate. Group activities are important. Through interaction with others you learn more.

Chapter 5 Reflection and Discussion Questions

o   What stands out for you in the student responses discussed in this chapter?

o   How do you expect your students would respond to learning about MI theory?

o   How do you expect your students would respond to MI-based learning activities?

o   How could you prepare them for MI-based practices?

REFERENCES

Armstrong, T. (1993). *Seven kinds of smart: Identifying and developing your many intelligences.* New York: Plume/Penguin.

Baum, S., Viens, J., & Slatin, B. (in press). *Multiple intelligences in the elementary classroom: Pathways to thoughtful practice.* New York: Teachers College Press.

Bickerton, R. (2000, June). Personal correspondence.

Campbell, B. (1994). *The multiple intelligences handbook: Lesson plans and more.* Stanwood, WA: Campbell & Associates.

Connecticut State Department of Education. (1997). Connecticut learns: School-to-career system. http://www.ctdol.state.ct.us/schtocar/school.htm.

Costanzo, M. (1997a). AMI teacher research report. Unpublished report.

Costanzo, M. (1997b). "How are you smart?" Unpublished raw data.

Coustan, T. (1998). AMI teacher research report. Unpublished report.

Dweck, C., & Elliott, E. S. (1983). Achievement motivation. In P. Mussen (Ed.), *Handbook of child psychology* (Vol. 4, 3rd ed., pp. 643–691). New York: Wiley.

Faculty of the New City School. (1994). *Celebrating multiple intelligences: Teaching for success.* St. Louis, MO: The New City School.

Gardner, H. (1983). *Frames of mind: The theory of multiple intelligences.* New York: Basic Books.

Gardner, H. (1993a). *Frames of mind: The theory of multiple intelligences* (10th anniversary ed.). New York: Basic Books.

Gardner, H. (1993b). *Multiple intelligences: The theory in practice.* New York: Basic Books.

Gardner, H. (1999). *Intelligence reframed: Multiple intelligences for the 21st century.* New York: Basic Books.

Gardner, H., & Checkley, K. (1997, September). "The first seven and the eighth: A conversation with Howard Gardner." *Educational Leadership, 55*(1), 8–13.

Gardner, H., Feldman, D. H., & Krechevsky, M. (Eds.). (1998). *Project Zero frameworks for early childhood education* (3 vols.). New York: Teachers College Press.

Gray, J. H., & Viens, J. (1994, Winter). The theory of multiple intelligences: Understanding cognitive diversity in school. *National Forum, 1*(LXXIV), 22–25.

Herrnstein, R., & Murray, C. (1994). *The bell curve.* New York: Free Press.

Jean, M. (1997). AMI teacher journal. Unpublished data.

Kallenbach, S., & Viens, J. (Eds.). (2001). *Multiple intelligences in practice: Teacher research reports from the Adult Multiple Intelligences Study.* Boston: National Center for the Study of Adult Learning and Literacy.

Kornhaber, M., & Fierros, E. (2000). Project SUMIT website [online]. http://www.pzweb.harvard.edu/SUMIT

Lazear, D. (1994). *Seven pathways of learning: Teaching students and parents about multiple intelligences.* Tucson, AZ: Zephyr Press.

Mantzaris, J. (1998). AMI teacher journal. Unpublished data.

Marlowe, D. (1997). AMI teacher research report. Unpublished report.

Martin, H. (1996). *Multiple intelligences in the mathematics classroom.* Arlington Heights, IL: SkyLight Professional Development.

Paxton, D. (1997). AMI teacher research report. Unpublished report.

Paxton, D. (1998). AMI teacher research report. Unpublished report.

Porter, C. R. (1993). *Meet Addy.* Middleton, WI: Pleasant Company Publications.

Rosnow, R., Skedler, A., Jaeger, M., & Rind, B. (1994). Intelligence and the epistemics of interpersonal acumen: Testing some implications of Gardner's theory. *Intelligence, 19,* 93–116.

Shearer, B. (1994). *Stepping stones: A MIDAS workbook for the multiple intelligences.* Kent, OH: Zephyr.

About the Authors and Contributors

The following individuals worked together to create this Sourcebook. Their biographies follow.

Adult Multiple Intelligences (AMI) Study Codirectors

Silja Kallenbach
New England Literacy Resource Center/
  World Education
44 Farnsworth Street
Boston, MA 02210, USA
617-482-9485
silja_kallenbach@worlded.org

Julie Viens
Project Zero
Harvard Graduate School of Education
124 Mount Auburn Street, Suite 500
Cambridge, MA 02138, USA
617-496-6574
julie@pz.harvard.edu

AMI Teacher–Researchers and Their Affiliations during the AMI Study

ABE = Adult Basic Education, GED = General Education Development, ESOL = English for Speakers of Other Languages

Elizabeth Cornwell	Family literacy instructor at the Learning Center at Region 9 in Rumford, Maine, and a past president of the Maine Music Teachers Association
Meg Costanzo	ABE, GED, and Diploma program teacher at The Tutorial Center in Manchester, Vermont, and a family literacy tutor trainer for Vermont Reading Partners
Terri Coustan	ESOL and family literacy teacher at International Institute of Rhode Island in Providence, Rhode Island, and president of the Rhode Island Adult Literacy Council
Bonnie Fortini	Program codirector and math/literacy teacher at Machias Adult and Community Education in Machias, Maine
Martha Jean	ABE and GED teacher at Community Action in Haverhill, Massachusetts, and coordinator of Northeast Young Adults With Learning Disabilities (YALD) Project
Jean Mantzaris	Guidance counselor and codirector at Wallingford Adult Education Learning Center in Connecticut
Dianne Marlowe	ABE and GED teacher at Area Cooperative Educational Services in New Haven, Connecticut
Diane Paxton	ESOL teacher at Bunker Hill Community College and Centro Latino, and a 1998 corecipient of the TESOL Research Interest Section/Newbury House Distinguished Research Award
Wendy Quiñones	Adult Secondary level teacher and associate program coordinator at Wellspring House in Gloucester, Massachusetts
Lezlie Rocka	ABE teacher at Dorcas Place Parent Literacy Center in Providence, Rhode Island

The AMI Study was a collaboration between Project Zero and the New England Literacy Resource Center/ World Education. It was one of several research projects conducted under the auspices of the National Center for the Study of Adult Learning and Literacy (NCSALL) at Harvard University in collaboration with World Education. NCSALL is funded under the educational research and development center programs, award number R309B60002, as administered by the Office for Education Research and Improvement–National Institute of Post-secondary Education, Libraries, and Lifelong Learning, United States Department of Education.

NCSALL, Harvard Graduate School of Education, 101 Nichols House, 7 Appian Way, Cambridge, MA 02138, 617-495-4843.

The Teachers

Betsy Cornwell

Research question: Will awareness of their own intelligence profiles help my students become more independent learners?

Betsy Cornwell since 1992 has been a traveling teacher, delivering ABE, GED, and ESOL instruction to adults in their homes in rural Maine. Her interest in multiple intelligences stemmed from her 20-year experience as a piano teacher and her observations of the many faces of musical talent. Betsy did her AMI research while a family literacy instructor at the Learning Center at Region 9 in Rumford, Maine.

Betsy's research project was motivated by a desire to gain a better understanding of why some seemingly motivated and capable students appeared to be unable or unwilling to do the academic work necessary to reach their own goals. She set out to assist her students in developing their intelligence profiles, expecting "the intelligence profiles to be a self-reflection tool that would help my students determine their most effective problem-solving techniques." She discovered that "what had appeared to be ineffective problem-solving techniques turned out to be a series of complex decisions and survival skills."

Betsy also found herself compelled to examine her own assumptions and values related to teaching and learning. She came to terms with the fact that, in many instances, her assumptions and values were different from those of her students. As she states, "Rather than forcing a student to choose between 'my way,' and 'your way,' I found that honoring my students' assumptions can be a starting point for expanding their understanding." This realization led her to seek and create other tools besides intelligence profiles to deal with student resistance and to help her students meet their basic needs for security and dignity while reaching their academic goals.

The AMI Study gave Betsy and her students the opportunity to explore together the relationships between multiple intelligences and the needs of the adult learner. The results were surprising and delightful to all concerned.

Meg Costanzo

Research question: How can teacher and student, working collaboratively, (a) identify the student's strongest intelligences through MI-based assessment and classroom activities and (b) use the understanding of these intelligences to guide the learning process?

Meg Costanzo began her work with adults in 1993, after "retiring" from a 23-year career as an elementary/middle school teacher. Meg did her AMI research while teaching students interested in earning their GED or Vermont Adult Diplomas at The Tutorial Center in Manchester, Vermont.

Meg's primary research concern was how to identify her students' strongest intelligences through an MI assessment in order to guide their learning process. She began her AMI journey by reflecting on her own intelligences and was then inspired to "encourage students to go through the same type of reflective process." Meg developed an assessment that students could use on their own and then encouraged her students to explore their intelligences in greater depth through weekly dialogue journals.

She discovered that "students appreciate having their intelligences acknowledged and valued. Many have never had the opportunity to claim their intelligences before this experience." In Meg's opinion, this deepened self-knowledge increased her students' self-confidence, which, in turn, increased the students' willingness to experiment with nontraditional learning strategies. However, she also emphasized the importance of providing repeated exposure to MI-based learning activities and strategies. She infused her teaching with MI-based approaches, especially project-based learning. Several quotes from her students substantiate her finding that "adult students are enthusiastic about real-life projects and are willing to take a role in how their learning programs are designed." Meg found that working from students' strengths led them to think more readily "outside of the box" and to become better and more confident problem solvers.

Terri Coustan

Research question: (a) What impact do ESOL activities informed by MI theory have on student engagement and learning strategies? (b) How do prior cultural learning and experiences shape students' reaction to and participation in ESOL activities informed by MI theory?

Teaching has been Terri Coustan's vocation and avocation since 1964. Terri began her career in New Haven, Connecticut, public schools as a language therapist and then as a Head Start teacher. She later worked as a drama coach, preschool teacher, assistant principal, and fifth-grade teacher in other cities.

Terri did her AMI research project while teaching ESOL at the International Institute of Rhode Island, in Providence, where she taught mostly Hmong students from Laos. Her research efforts focused on how to use MI theory in her ESOL classroom in ways that enhanced student engagement and learning.

Terri's approach was twofold. Through a synthesis of her informal observations of her students, she developed an understanding of their MI-related strengths and learning strategies. She then designed classroom activities that were geared to those strengths and strategies she had observed. She created alternative "entry points" into the material that gave students ways of learning and expressing their understanding beyond verbal means.

Terri found that the MI-informed choice activities aided her students' academic progress. Although she found that her students had difficulty understanding MI theory and were not able to identify their more specific learning strategies, they did improve their ability to reflect on their own learning. Having worked with the same group, more or less, for the previous 3 years, Terri attributed her findings to her implementation of an MI-informed approach, the one significant change in her classroom.

Interestingly, Terri also found that giving students choices in a nonthreatening learning environment resulted in students' taking greater control in the classroom and expanding their cultural norms for classroom behavior. Terri credits her MI-inspired activities for fostering student participation and assertiveness, a stark contrast to 3 years of relative student passivity.

Bonnie Fortini

Research question: What kind of MI-informed instruction and assessment can be developed that will help adult learners deal with math anxiety, so they may reach their stated goals?

Bonnie Fortini, after moving "Downeast" to Machias, Maine, began working with the adult education program there in 1990 as a literacy tutor while helping her family establish a small specialty fiber farm.

Bonnie conducted her AMI research as a math/literacy teacher at Machias Adult and Community Education. Her research centered on exploring ways in which MI-based applications could alleviate her students' math anxiety. Her hypothesis was that knowledge about their own intelligence strengths would enable her students to develop better learning strategies, which, in turn, would combat math anxiety. She used a visual representation of math anxiety as well as a survey to help her students analyze and talk about their own experience. She also infused her teaching with MI self-assessments and related discussions about MI theory.

To a lesser extent, Bonnie designed MI-based lessons. In this she felt constrained by her students' traditional expectations and her own teaching preferences and intelligence strengths. Nevertheless, the few MI-based lessons she did drew positive comments from several students. Bonnie found that

> The introduction of MI theory and the survey-generated illustration of our unique profiles of intelligences seemed to facilitate conversation among students about issues of education, even the more sensitive issues like learning difficulties and math anxiety. Perhaps the opportunity to recognize that each person is a complex collection of strengths and weaknesses created a comfort level that allowed students to open up.

In the end, Bonnie concluded that

> Although students' discussions of MI, their own strengths, and math anxiety do not necessarily imply that MI helped alleviate math anxiety, they did provide the first step in that direction. MI showed itself to be an excellent point of departure for thinking about math anxiety and how students can work to overcome it.

Bonnie describes the AMI Study as a truly exciting and energizing experience. Her participation broadened her knowledge about learning and validated and enriched her efforts as a teacher and administrator.

Martha Jean

Research question: Can MI-informed lessons help the progress and attendance of ADD and LD students preparing for the GED?

Martha Jean has taught GED and basic education classes for the homeless since 1990. She also has served as the coordinator of the Northeast Young Adults With Learning Disabilities Project, which gave her a special interest in helping adults who have difficulty learning. In her experience, these students tended to have poor attendance and made little progress.

In her AMI research, Martha designed and implemented MI-informed lessons for GED students. Martha's challenge was to develop an approach that accounted for the diversity of students' intelligences and possible approaches represented in MI theory while addressing the requirements of the GED test.

Martha addressed her question by developing four types of MI-based experiences: (a) activities to introduce students to MI theory, (b) "warm-up" activities, (c) topic-based whole-group activities, and (d) Choose 3 activities. Martha used the introductory activities as a rationale for the practices in her classroom and to ensure that students understood they each have a unique profile of intelligences that they can tap to prepare for the GED. "Warm-up" activities were enjoyable experiences that helped prepare students to do the more tedious tasks. Whole-group activities were meant to teach specific skills or topics, for example, map reading. The heart of Martha's approach was Choose 3 activities. Martha chose a GED topic, such as measurement, or planets, or editorial cartoons, and developed about nine activities, among which students chose three to complete.

Martha's findings bear out the value of an MI-informed approach to GED preparation, particularly for ADD or LD students. These students responded overwhelmingly favorably to the MI-informed activities. In fact, their attendance proved to be significantly better than that of the students in Martha's non-MI-informed classes. Martha's data also demonstrated greater progress toward GED preparation for ADD or LD students.

Although Martha's findings strongly suggest the benefits of an MI-informed approach, Martha found that whether or how MI theory is applied depends on where students are in the GED preparation process. Namely, as students approach GED readiness, their studies need to narrow to specific GED content and to discrete test-taking skills away from the broad themes of Choose 3 activities.

Jean Mantzaris

Research question: How will Adult Diploma students' awareness of their own intelligences and their participation in activities informed by MI theory affect their career decision-making process?

Jean Mantzaris is a veteran counselor of adults in community college and adult education programs. She joined the AMI Study in the fall of 1997 while working as a full-time guidance counselor of high school preparation and ESOL students at the Wallingford Adult Education Learning Center in Connecticut.

The AMI Study was an opportunity for Jean to add another dimension to her career counseling work. She wanted to help her students to pursue careers that matched their intelligence strengths and interests. Jean's research focused on how students' awareness of and participation in MI activities would affect their career choices.

Jean infused her career awareness class with MI-based activities and invited her students to explore their multiple intelligences. For example, in an effort to "dig deep" into each student's intelligence profile, Jean asked the students to reflect on the activities they loved to do as children and to bring representations of these activities into class. She then invited students to consider a possible connection between their childhood preferences and the intelligences they had identified in the class as adults. Through this and other MI-based activities, students became more aware and appreciative of their own and each other's strengths. Jean also observed a "notable increase in student engagement, motivation, camaraderie, and persistence."

Analysis of student comments and their plans for next career steps led Jean to conclude that awareness of their own intelligences influenced students to broaden their career decision-making to be more aligned with their intelligences. "Once students became aware of their strengths, possibilities of new careers abounded." This more complex understanding of their own strengths and the career possibilities that might best correspond to them resulted in students' extending their career exploration rather than identifying an immediate job choice. This proved to be a double-edged sword for some students who were under pressure to take any job.

Dianne Marlowe

Research question: What will happen when I use MI theory to inform the teaching of math?

Dianne Marlowe taught ABE, GED, and computer classes at Area Cooperative Educational Services (ACES) in New Haven, Connecticut, for almost 14 years. She conducted her AMI research while teaching math at ACES until the program closed in 1997.

Dianne's work with the AMI Study focused on problem-solving in the math classroom. Many of the students who had returned to school expressed anxiety about math, having had negative experiences in the past. She hoped that MI-informed teaching approaches would facilitate math learning.

Dianne's project used quilting to teach geometric concepts and formulas. Students made tangram patterns and then computed areas and perimeters for each of the polygons. Then each student designed and sewed a quilt square, enlarging polygon shapes cut from their original tangram. Dianne integrated literature and writing into the quilting activity, making the curriculum truly interdisciplinary. As new students entered the class, the other students taught them about MI and oriented them to the project.

At first, Dianne's students were resistant to MI-based learning. They worried they would not learn what they needed to know to pass the GED test. Dianne speculated that a teacher-directed class felt safer to them; student-centered activities seemed less predictable and represented more of a risk. It did not take long, however, for her students, including the men, to become fully engaged in the quilting project. After the project was completed, Dianne said her students felt proud of their creativity and abilities, and felt they had learned a great deal. One student, who initially was extremely resistant, and who earned his GED during the quilting project, said he would never forget the geometry formulas he learned as part of the project.

Dianne discovered that students learn best when they have choices and can demonstrate their knowledge using their strongest intelligences. She found that the MI definition of intelligence as a way of solving a problem and/or creating a product can be used to make education relevant and engaging for adult learners. Her students gained new vocabulary with which to name their areas of strength. Dianne believes that her MI-based project afforded every student many opportunities to succeed and flourish.

Diane Paxton

Research question: What effect does metacognitive awareness of their own multiple intelligences have on the perceptions of effective ESOL teaching and learning by students with limited native language literacy? What happens when I try to integrate MI into an ESOL class?

Diane Paxton's work in adult education has focused on literacy and language development with adult immigrants who are speakers of other languages. She has taught in community-based organizations, housing projects, and community colleges. During her AMI research, she taught ESOL at Centro Hispano in Chelsea, Massachusetts, and at Bunker Hill Community College in Boston.

Diane's AMI work involved using MI theory to design creative activities and corresponding assessment tools toward the goal of more effective learning and building greater student acceptance of nontraditional approaches. Diane's students reflected regularly on their progress and likes and dislikes related to the various learning activities. Diane's challenge was to consider how MI theory can inform her teaching in new ways, and in ways that did not interfere or contradict her already well-grounded practice as an ESOL instructor.

Like many students, Diane's students initially resisted MI-based approaches, seeing them as unusual, childish, or simply too different from the traditional approaches they knew and had come to expect. Interestingly, Diane herself resisted MI. She found the notion of assessing students' intelligences problematic. Once she recognized that assessing students' intelligences is neither necessary nor prescribed by the theory, Diane used MI theory in many creative ways to further enhance her multimodal approach to teaching English. Over time, her students' perceptions of effective ESOL teaching and learning changed. The students accepted and, for the most part, became enthusiastic about diverse ways of learning English.

Diane accounted for her students' changed perceptions in several ways. She writes, "The development of the students' ability to think about and articulate their ideas about how they like to learn is the result of our ongoing assessments.... Building opportunities to raise metacognitive awareness in the class helped the MI activities have a more positive effect with these groups of students." Diane also noted that developing a sense of community in the classroom was important in students' acceptance and ultimate enthusiasm for the nontraditional approaches.

Wendy Quiñones

Research question: Will the use of a multiple intelligences framework support the goals and practices of popular education in an ABE classroom?

Wendy Quiñones has taught adults in a variety of settings since 1988, with a primary interest in empowering them personally, in their communities, and in their society. While an AMI teacher–researcher, Wendy taught women in a nontraditional education program, Wellspring House in Gloucester, Massachusetts, that helped them both to strengthen their academic skills and to identify their life goals. As an AMI researcher, Wendy explored whether MI theory might enhance her teaching that was based on the popular education approach where the overarching goal is social action.

Wendy considered the key aspects of popular education, such as developing self-respect and respect toward others, creating an environment based on democratic principles, and using nontraditional and problem-posing pedagogical approaches. Toward those ends, Wendy facilitated students' self-assessment and recognition of their own and their peers' intelligence strengths. She created opportunities for student choice and decision-making in the classroom, and integrated more hands-on and real world activities in her teaching. Perhaps the highlight of her MI-informed activities was giving students opportunities to demonstrate their understanding of key concepts through MI-informed projects of their choosing.

Wendy's hunch of a "natural fit" between MI-informed approaches and popular education was validated in her study. She found that MI theory supported her efforts in ways that enhanced her teaching methods and popular education-based goals. She identified four related findings. Using an MI-informed approach: (a) helped her align her teaching more closely to popular education principles, (b) created empowering opportunities for students, (c) promoted a more democratic classroom environment, and (d) served to increase students' positive sense of self and appreciation of others.

Through her efforts on the AMI Study, Wendy discovered that it was not only her students who had been powerfully affected: "I feel that both my understanding and my practice have been transformed, and that as a result I am much closer to the kind of teacher I want to be than I was just 18 months ago."

Lezlie Rocka

Research question: How does knowledge of MI theory broaden a multisensory approach to the teaching of reading and writing?

Lezlie Rocka applied to be part of the AMI Study with Louise Cherubini when they both worked at Dorcas Place Parent Literacy Center in Providence, Rhode Island. MI theory sounded compatible with their interest in multisensory teaching. Louise was Lezlie's mentor in using a multisensory approach with her limited literacy students. They hoped the project would broaden the scope of techniques they used with their students. Louise participated for the first 6 months, and Lezlie continued the teacher research on her own for the remaining 12 months.

Lezlie's research project was driven by a quest to understand whether MI theory has something to offer to a multisensory approach to teaching reading and writing at the low-intermediate level. When Lezlie compared lessons that were designed using a multisensory approach to those that integrated MI theory, she realized that multisensory teaching uses the senses to impart information, but it does not entail choices for students to express their understanding. She began to give her students choices as part of the reading comprehension component of her curriculum. As Lezlie explains,

> We thought that if students were expressing and processing the information in as many ways as possible, this would assist them in using their strongest intelligences to understand the information.... We began to consistently create lessons that were more interactive and action oriented. Students worked together, gave presentations, acted in skits, organized presentation charts, drew or sculpted scenes, and so on They seemed to comprehend the writing well enough that they could teach it to others.

The choice-based activities allowed Lezlie a much better view of her students' reading comprehension and strategies. Her teacher research led her to the conclusion that "the application of MI theory in my reading lessons seemed to cause improvements in specific reading strategies, comprehension, retention, and interest in the reading." She noted that this progress was true for all but two of her students, whom she suspected of having severe learning disabilities. At the end of her research project, she was pleased to find that MI did help to broaden her approach to teaching reading.

The AMI Study Codirectors

Julie Viens

Julie Viens has been a researcher with Project Zero since 1988, working on several projects related to the educational application of multiple intelligences theory. Julie's disappointment with her high school experience aroused her interest in and pursuit of "alternative education." Her experimental undergraduate program gave her the more personalized approaches she sought, while deepening her understanding of teaching and learning that was "in the spirit" of MI theory. Two years after graduating, Julie joined the Project Zero team. The AMI Study represents Julie's first foray into adult education. She has felt privileged to learn so much about MI and adult education from and with this group of inquisitive and energetic women.

Julie also works as a consultant to schools and programs that are adopting MI theory and practices. She is coauthor of *Building on Children's Strengths: The Experiences of Project Spectrum*, which outlines a 10-year project at Project Zero using MI theory in early education. Julie is currently working on *Multiple Intelligences in the Elementary Classroom: Pathways to Thoughtful Practice*, a professional development guide that presents five "pathways" through which to understand and apply multiple intelligences theory.

Silja Kallenbach

Silja Kallenbach has worked in adult education since 1981 as a teacher, administrator, and staff developer. Silja has directed the New England Literacy Resource Center at World Education in Boston since 1994. She is the publisher of and a writer for NELRC's Change Agent newspaper, whose goal is to inspire and enable adult literacy teachers and students to make civic participation and social-justice-related concerns part of their teaching and learning. She was a coresearcher on the national Equipped For the Future (EFF) lifelong learning content standards project.

Silja has presented workshops and seminars on numerous topics related to adult literacy education, fundraising, and organizational development. She is the cofounder and former associate director of the Boston Adult Literacy Fund. From 1985 to 1988, she served as the director of the Boston Adult Literacy Initiative.

AMI RESOURCES TO DOWNLOAD

The following AMI resources are available on the web site of the National Center for the Study of Adult Learning and Literacy (NCSALL) http://ncsall.gse.harvard.edu

Focus on Basics is NCSALL's quarterly journal that presents best practices, current research on adult learning and literacy, and how research is used by adult basic education teachers, counselors, program administrators, and policymakers. Vol. 3, Issue 8, March 1999, focuses on the AMI Study.

MI Annotated Bibliography contains 46 entries divided into three categories: MI Theory, MI Research Projects, and MI Practices, published in 2001.

Multiple Intelligences in Practice: Teacher Research Reports From the Adult Multiple Intelligences Study, published in 2001, contains Teacher Research Reports from nine AMI teachers with an introductory chapter by the study's codirectors.

Open to Interpretation: Multiple Intelligences Theory in Adult Literacy Education is the AMI research report, published in 2002. The AMI Study investigated the question: How can MI theory support instruction and assessment in Adult Basic Education, Adult Secondary Education, and English for Speakers of Other Languages?

Additional resources are available on the AMI web site at http://pzweb.harvard.edu/ami

 **INDEX**